Irish Witchcraft and Demonology

CHAPTER IX... 125
   A.D. 1807 TO PRESENT DAY
      MARY BUTTERS, THE CARNMONEY WITCH—BALLAD ON HER—THE HAND OF GLORY—A JOURNEY THROUGH THE AIR—A "WITCH" IN 1911—SOME MODERN ILLUSTRATIONS OF CATTLE- AND MILK-MAGIC—TRANSFERENCE OF DISEASE BY A cailleach—BURYING THE. SHEAF—J.P.'S COMMISSION—CONCLUSION

CHAPTER I

SOME REMARKS ON WITCHCRAFT IN IRELAND

IT is said, though we cannot vouch for the accuracy of the statement, that in a certain book on the natural history of Ireland there occurs a remarkable and oft-quoted chapter on Snakes—the said chapter consisting of the words, "There are no snakes in Ireland." In the opinion of most people at the present day a book on Witchcraft in Ireland would be of equal length and similarly worded, except for the inclusion of the Kyteler case in the town of Kilkenny in the first half of the fourteenth century. For, with the exception of that classic incident, modern writers seem to hold that the witch-cult never found a home in Ireland as it did elsewhere. For example, the article on "Witchcraft" in the latest edition of the *Encyclopædia Britannica* mentions England and Scotland, then passes on to the Continent, and altogether ignores this country; and this is, in general, the attitude adopted by writers on the subject. In view of this it seems very strange that no one has attempted to show why the Green Isle was so especially favoured above the rest of the civilised world, or how it was that it alone escaped the contracting of a disease that not for years but for centuries had infected Europe to the core. As it happens they may spare themselves the labour of seeking for an explanation of Ireland's exemption, for we hope to show that the belief in witchcraft reached the country, and took a fairly firm hold there, though by no means to the extent that it did in Scotland and England. The subject has never been treated of fully before, though isolated notices may be found here and there; this book, however imperfect it may be, can fairly claim to be the first attempt to collect the scattered stories and records of witchcraft in Ireland from many out-of-the-way sources, and to present them when collected in a concise and palatable form. Although the volume may furnish little or nothing new to the history or psychology of witchcraft in general, yet it may also claim to be an unwritten chapter in Irish history, and to show that in this respect a considerable portion of our country fell into line with the rest of Europe.

At the outset the plan and scope of this book must be made clear. It will be noticed that the belief in fairies and suchlike beings is hardly touched upon at all, except in those instances where fairy lore and witchcraft become inextricably blended.

The reason for this method of treatment is not hard to find. From the Anglo-Norman invasion down the country has been divided into two opposing elements, the Celtic and the English. It is true that on many occasions these coalesced in peace and war, in religion and politics, but as a rule they were distinct, and this became even more marked after the spread of the Reformation. It was therefore in the Anglo-Norman (and subsequently in the Protestant) portion of the country that we find the development of witchcraft along similar lines to those in England or the Continent, and it is with this that we are dealing in this book; the Celtic element had its own superstitious beliefs, but these never developed in this direction. In England and Scotland during the mediæval and later periods of its existence witchcraft was an offence against the laws of God and man; in Celtic Ireland dealings with the unseen were not regarded with such abhorrence, and indeed had the sanction of custom and antiquity. In England after the Reformation we seldom find members of the Roman Catholic Church taking any prominent part in witch cases, and this is equally true of Ireland from the same date. Witchcraft seems to have been confined m the Protestant party, as far as we can judge from the material at our disposal, while it is probable that the existence of the penal laws (active or quiescent) would deter the Roman Catholics from coming into any prominence in a matter which would be likely to attract public attention to itself in such a marked degree. A certain amount of capital has been made by some partisan writers out of this, but to imagine that the ordinary Roman Catholic of, let us say, the seventeenth century, was one whit less credulous or superstitious than Protestant peers, bishops, or judges, would indeed be to form a conception directly at variance with experience and common sense. Both parties had their beliefs, but they followed different channels, and affected public life in different ways.

Another point with reverence to the plan of this work as indicated by the title needs a few words of explanation. It will be seen by the reader that the volume does not deal solely with the question of witchcraft, though that we have endeavoured to bring into prominence as much as possible, but that tales of the supernatural, of the appearance of ghosts, and of the Devil, are also included, especially in chapters IV and VI. If we have erred in inserting these, we have at least erred in the respectable company of Sir Walter Scott, C. K. Sharpe, and other writers of note. We have included them, partly because they afford interesting reading, and are culled from sources with which the average reader is unacquainted, but principally because they reflect as in a mirror the temper of the age, and show the degree to which every class of Society was permeated with the belief in the grosser forms of the supernatural, and the blind readiness with which it accepted what would at the present day be tossed aside as unworthy of even a cursory examination. This is forcibly brought out in the instance of a lawsuit being undertaken at the instigation of a ghost—a quaint item of legal lore. The judge who adjudicated, or the jury and lawyers who took their respective parts in such a case, would with equal readiness have tried and found guilty a person on the charge of witchcraft; and probably did so far oftener than we are aware of.

The question will naturally be asked by the reader—what reason can be offered for Ireland's comparative freedom from the scourge, when the whole of Europe was so sorely lashed for centuries? It is difficult fully to account for it, but the consideration of the following points affords a partial explanation.

In the first place Ireland's aloofness may be alleged as a reason. The "Emerald Gem of the Western World" lies far away on the verge of Ocean, remote from those influences which so profoundly affected popular thought in other countries. It is a truism to say that it has been separated from England and the Continent by more than geographical features, or that in many respects, in its ecclesiastical organisation, its literature, and so on, it has developed along semi-independent lines. And so, on account of this remoteness. it would seem to have been prevented from acquiring and assimilating the varying and complex features which went to make up the witchcraft conception. Or, to put it in other words, mediæval witchcraft was a byproduct of the civilisation of the Roman Empire. Ireland's civilisation developed along other and more barbaric lines, and so had no opportunity of assimilating the particular phases of that belief which obtained elsewhere in Europe.

Consequently, when the Anglo-Normans came over, they found that the native Celts had no predisposition towards accepting the view of the witch as an emissary of Satan and an enemy of the Church, though they fully believed in supernatural influences of both good and evil, and credited their Bards and Druids with the possession of powers beyond the ordinary. Had this country never suffered a cross-channel invasion, had she been left to work out her destiny unaided and uninfluenced by her neighbours, it is quite conceivable that at some period in her history she would have imbibed the witchcraft spirit, and, with the genius characteristic of her, would have blended it with her own older beliefs, and so would have ultimately evolved a form of that creed which would have differed in many points from what was held elsewhere. As it happens, the English and their successors had the monopoly, and retained it in their own hands; thus the Anglo-Norman invaders may be given the credit of having been the principal means of preventing the growth and spread of witchcraft in Celtic Ireland.

Another point arises in connection with the advance of the Reformation in Ireland. Unfortunately the persecution of witches did not cease in the countries where that movement made headway—far from it; on the contrary it was kept up with unabated vigour. Infallibility was transferred from the Church to the Bible; the Roman Catholic persecuted the witch because Supreme Pontiffs had stigmatised her as a heretic and an associate of Satan, while the Protestant acted similarly because Holy Writ contained the grim command "Thou shalt not suffer a witch to live." Thus persecution flourished equally in Protestant and Roman Catholic kingdoms. But in Ireland the conditions were different. We find there a Roman Catholic majority, not racially predisposed towards such a belief, debarred by their religious and political opinions from taking their full share in public affairs, and opposed in every way to the Protestant minority. The consequent turmoil and clash of war gave no opportunity for the witchcraft idea to come to maturity and cast its seeds broadcast; it was trampled into the earth by the feet of the combatants, and, though the minority believed firmly in witchcraft and kindred subjects, it had not sufficient strength to make the belief general throughout the country.

A third reason that may be brought forward to account for the comparative immunity of Ireland was the total absence of literature on the subject. The diffusion of books and pamphlets throughout a country or district is one of the recognised ways of propagating any particular creed; the friends and opponents of Christianity have equally recognised the truth of this, and have always utilised it to the fullest extent. Now in England from the sixteenth century we find an enormous literary output relative to witchcraft, the majority of the works being in support of that belief. Many of these were small pamphlets, which served as the "yellow press" of the day; they were well calculated to arouse the superstitious feelings of their readers, as they were written from a sensational standpoint—indeed it seems very probable that the compilers, in their desire to produce a startling catch-penny which would be sure to have a wide circulation, occasionally drew upon their imaginations for their facts. The evil that was wrought by such amongst an ignorant and superstitious people can well be imagined; unbelievers would be converted, while the credulous would be rendered more secure in their credulity.

At a later date, when men had become practical enough to question the reality of such things, a literary war took place, and in this "battle of the books" we find such well-known names as Richard Baxter, John Locke, Meric Casaubon, Joseph Glanvil, and Francis Hutchinson, ranged on one side or the other. Thus the ordinary Englishman would have no reasonable grounds for being ignorant of the power of witches, or of the various opinions held relative to them. In Ireland, on the other hand (with the solitary exception of a pamphlet of 1699, which may or may not have been locally printed), there is not the slightest trace of any witchcraft literature being published in the country until we reach the opening years of the nineteenth century. All our information therefore with respect to Ireland comes from incidental notices in books and from sources across the water. We might with reason expect that the important trial of Florence Newton at Youghal in 1661, concerning the historical reality of which there can be no possible doubt, would be immortalised by Irish writers and publishers, but as a matter of fact it is only preserved for us in two London printed books. There is no confusion between cause and effect; books on witchcraft would, naturally, be the result of witch-trials, but in their turn they would be the means of spreading the idea and of introducing it to the notice of people who otherwise might never have shown the least interest in the matter. Thus the absence of this form of literature in Ireland seriously hindered the advance of the belief in (and consequent practice of) witchcraft.

When did witchcraft make its appearance in Ireland, and what was its progress therein? It seems probable that this belief, together with certain aspects of fairy lore hitherto unknown to the Irish, and ideas relative to milk and butter magic, may in the main be counted as results of the Anglo-Norman invasion, though it is possible that an earlier instalment of these came in with the Scandinavians. With our present knowledge we cannot trace its active existence in Ireland further back than the Kyteler case of 1324; and this, though it was almost certainly the first occasion on which the evil made itself apparent to the general public, yet seems to have been only the culmination of events that had been quietly and unobtrusively happening for some little time previously. The language used by the Parliament with reference to the case of 1447 would lead us to infer that nothing remarkable or worthy of note in the way of witchcraft or sorcery had occurred in the country during the intervening century and a quarter. For another hundred years nothing is recorded, while the second half of the sixteenth century furnishes us with two cases and a suggestion of several others.

It is stated by some writers (on the authority, we believe, of an early editor of *Hudibras*) that during the rule of the Commonwealth Parliament *thirty thousand* witches were put to death in England. Others, possessing a little common sense, place the number at three thousand, but even this is far too high. Yet it seems to be beyond all doubt that more witches were sent to the gallows at that particular period than at any other in English history. Ireland seems to have escaped scot-free—at least we have not been able to find any instances recorded of witch trials at that time. Probably the terribly disturbed state of the country, the tremendous upheaval of the Cromwellian confiscations, and the various difficulties and dangers experienced by the new settlers would largely account for this immunity.

Dr. Notestein [1] shows that the tales of apparitions and devils, of knockings and strange noises, with which English popular literature of the period is filled, are indications of a very overwrought public mind; of similar stories in Ireland, also indicative of a similar state of tension, some examples are given in chapter IV. Though the first half of the seventeenth century is so barren with respect to *witchcraft*, yet it should be noticed that during that period we come across frequent notices of ghosts, apparitions, devils, &c., which forces us to the conclusion that the increase of the belief in such subjects at that time was almost entirely due to the advent of the Cromwellian settlers and the Scotch colonists in Ulster; indeed the beliefs of the latter made the Northern Province a miniature Scotland in this respect. We cannot blame them for this; could anything else be expected from men who, clergy and laity alike, were saturated with the superstitions that were then so prominent in the two countries from which their ranks had been recruited?

Thus the seventeenth century was the period *par excellence* of witchcraft, demonology, and the supernatural in Ireland. The most remarkable witch case of that time, the trial of Florence Newton in 1661, to which allusion has already been made, seems to have been largely influenced by what occurred in England, while the various methods suggested or employed as a test of that old woman's culpability are quite in accordance with the procedure adopted a few years previously by the English witch-finder general, the infamous Matthew Hopkins. After 1711 the period of decadence is reached, while between that date and 1808 nothing has been found, though it may be safely inferred that that blank was filled by incidents similar to the case of Mar Butters and others, as described in the final chapter; and possibly too, as in England, by savage outbursts on the part of the ignorant and credulous multitude.

Witchcraft never flourished to any great extent in Ireland, nor did anything ever occur which was worthy of the name of persecution-except perhaps as a sequel to the Kyteler case, and the details of which we fear will never be recovered. The first part of this statement must be taken generally and not pressed too closely, as it is based almost entirely on negative evidence, *i.e.* the absence of information on the subject. England has a lengthy list of books and pamphlets, while Scotland's share in the business may be learnt from the fine series of criminal trials edited by Pitcairn in. the Miscellanies of the Abbotsford Club, not to speak of other works; notwithstanding these, many cases in both England and Scotland must have been unrecorded. Ireland can produce nothing like this, for, as we have already shown, all *printed* notices of Irish witchcraft, with one possible exception, are recorded in books published outside the country. Nevertheless, if all likely sources, both in MS. and print, could be searched, it is highly probable that a much fuller volume than the present one could be written on the subject. The Elizabethan Act was passed on account of cases (recorded and unrecorded) that had arisen in the country; while, human nature being what it is, it seems likely that the very passing of that Statute by the Irish Parliament was in itself a sufficient incentive to the witches to practise their art. No belief really gains ground until it is forbidden; then the martyrs play their part, and there is a consequent increase in the number of the followers.

The Act of 1634 shows the opinion that was entertained in the highest circles relative to the baneful influence of witches and the menace their presence was to the safety of the community at large; in this no doubt the effect of the "evil eye," or of the satirical verses of Bards, would be equally classed with witchcraft proper.

From various hints and incidental notices, such as in the account of the bewitching of Sir George Pollock, or in Law's statement relative to the case of Mr. Moor, as well as from a consideration of the prevalence of the belief amongst all classes of society, it may be inferred that far more cases of witchcraft occurred in Ireland during the sixteenth and seventeenth centuries than one imagines, though in comparison with other countries their numbers would be but small. Future students of old documents may be able to bear out this statement, and to supply information at present unavailable.

To deal with the subject of witchcraft in general, with its psychology or with the many strange items which it included, would be out of place in a work exclusively devoted to one particular country, nor indeed could it be adequately dealt with in the space at our disposal; it is necessary, however, to say a few words on the matter in order to show by comparison how much pain and unhappiness the people of Ireland escaped through the non-prevalence of this terrible cult amongst them.

In the first place, to judge from the few witch-trials recorded, it may be claimed that torture as a means of extracting evidence was never used upon witches in Ireland (excepting the treatment of Petronilla of Meath by Bishop de Ledrede, which seems to have been carried out is in what may be termed a purely unofficial manner). It would be interesting indeed to work through the extant Records for the purpose of seeing how often torture was judicially used on criminals in Ireland, and probably the student who undertakes the investigation will find that this terrible and illogical method of extracting the truth (!) was very seldom utilised. Nor is it at all clear that torture was employed in England in similar trials. Dr. Notestein [2] thinks that there are some traces of it, which cannot however be certainly proved, except in one particular instance towards the end of the reign of James I, though this was for the exceptional crime of practising sorcery (and therefore high treason) against that too credulous king. Was its use ever legalised by Act of Parliament in either country?

In Scotland, on the other hand, it was employed with terrible frequency; there was hardly a trial for witchcraft or sorcery but some of the unfortunates incriminated were subjected to this terrible ordeal. Even as late as 1690 torture was judicially applied to extract evidence, for in that year a Jacobite gentleman was questioned by the boots. But Scotland, even at its worst, fades into insignificance before certain parts of the Continent, where torture was used to an extent and degree that can only be termed hellish; the appalling ingenuity displayed in the various methods of applying the "question extraordinary" seems the work of demons rather than of Christians, and makes one blush for humanity. The *repetition* of torture was forbidden, indeed, but the infamous Inquisitor, James Sprenger, imagined a subtle distinction by which each fresh application was a *continuation* and not a repetition of the first; one sorceress in Germany suffered this continuation no less, than *fifty-six* times.

Nor was the punishment of death by fire for witchcraft or sorcery employed to any extent in Ireland. We have one undoubted instance, and a general hint of' some others as a sequel to this. How the two witches were put to death in 1578 we are not told, but probably it was by hanging. Subsequent to the passing of the Act of 1586 the method of execution would have been that for felony. On the Continent the stake was in continual request. In 1514 three hundred persons were burnt alive for this crime at Como. Between 1615 and 1635 more than six thousand sorcerers were burnt in the diocese of Strasburg, while, if we can credit the figures of Bartholomew de Spina, in Lombardy a thousand sorcerers a year were put to death *for the space of twenty-five years.* [3] The total number of persons executed in various ways for this crime has, according to the *Encyclopædia Britannica*, been variously estimated at from one hundred thousand to several millions; if the latter figure be too high undoubtedly the former is far too low.

In the persecution of those who practised magical arts no rank or class in society was spared; the noble equally with the peasant was liable to torture and death. This was especially true of the earlier stages of the movement when *sorcery* rather than *witchcraft* was the crime committed. For there is a general distinction between the two, though in many instances they are confounded. Sorcery was, so to speak, more of an aristocratic pursuit; the sorcerer was the master of the Devil (until his allotted time expired), and compelled him to do his bidding: the witch generally belonged to the lower classes, embodied in her art many practices which lay on the borderland between good and evil, and was rather the slave of Satan, who almost invariably proved to be a most faithless and unreliable employer. For an illustration from this country of the broad distinction between the two the reader may compare Dame Alice Kyteler with Florence Newton. Anybody might become a victim of the witch epidemic; noblemen, scholars, monks, nuns, titled ladies, bishops, clergy—none were immune from accusation and condemnation. Nay, even a saint once fell under suspicion; in 1595 S. Francis de Sales was accused of having been present at a sorcerers' sabbath, and narrowly escaped being burnt by the populace. [4] Much more might be written in the same strain, but sufficient illustrations have been brought forward to show the reader that in its comparative immunity from witchcraft and its terrible consequences Ireland, generally deemed so unhappy, may be counted the most fortunate country in Europe.

In conclusion, we have not considered it necessary to append a bibliography. The books that have been consulted and which have contained no information relative to Ireland are, unfortunately, all too numerous, while those that have proved of use are fully referred to in the text or footnotes of the present volume. We should like however to acknowledge our indebtedness to such general works on the subject as Sir Walter Scott's *Demonology and Witchcraft*, C. K. Sharpe's *History of Witchcraft in Scotland*, John Ashton's *The Devil in Britain and America*, and Professor Wallace Notestein's *History of Witchcraft in England*, 1558-1718 (Washington, 1911); the last three contain most useful bibliographical notices. Much valuable information with respect to the traditional versions of certain incidents which occurred in Ulster has been gleaned from Classon Porter's pamphlet,

Witches, Warlocks, and Ghosts (reprinted from *The Northern Whig* of 1885). For a good bird's-eye view of witchcraft on the Continent from the earliest times we can recommend J. Français' *L'église et la Sorcellerie* (Paris: Nourry, 1910).

Footnotes

1. In his *History of Witchcraft in England*.
2. Notestein, 10. *op. cit.*
3. Français, *L'église et la Sorcellerie*.
4. Français, *op. cit.*

CHAPTER II

A.D. 1324

DAME ALICE KYTELER, THE SORCERESS OF KILKENNY

THE history of the proceedings against Dame Alice Kyteler and her confederates on account of their dealings in unhallowed arts is to be found in a MS. in the British Museum, and has been edited amongst the publications of the Camden Society by Thomas Wright, who considers it to be a contemporary narrative. Good modern accounts of it are given in the same learned antiquary's "Narratives of Witchcraft and Sorcery" in *Transactions of the Ossory Archæological Society*, vol. i., and in the Rev. Dr. Carrigan's *History of the Diocese of Ossory*, vol. i.

Dame Alice Kyteler (such apparently being her maiden name), the *facile princeps* of Irish witches, was a member of a good Anglo-Norman family that had been settled in the city of Kilkenny for many ears. The coffin-shaped tombstone of one of her ancestors, Jose de Keteller, who died in 128-, is preserved at S. Mary's church; the inscription is in Norman-French and the lettering is Lombardic. The lady in question must have been far removed from the popular conception of a witch as an old woman of striking ugliness, or else her powers of attraction were very remarkable, for she had succeeded in leading four husbands to the altar. She had been married, first, to William Outlawe of Kilkenny, banker; secondly, to Adam le Blund of Callan; thirdly, to Richard de Valle—all of whom she was supposed to have got rid of by poison; and fourthly, to Sir John le Poer, whom it was said she deprived of his natural senses by philtres and incantations.

The Bishop of Ossory at this period was Richard de Ledrede, a Franciscan friar, and an Englishman by birth. He soon learnt that things were not as they should be, for when making a visitation of his diocese early in 1324 he found by an Inquisition, in which were five knights and numerous nobles, that there was in the city a band of heretical sorcerers, at the head of whom was Dame Alice. The following charges were laid against them.

1. They had denied the faith of Christ absolutely for a year or a month, according as the object they desired to gain through sorcery was of greater or less importance. During all that period they believed in none of the doctrines of the Church; they did not adore the Body of Christ, nor enter a sacred building to hear mass, nor make use of consecrated bread or holy water.
2. They offered in sacrifice to demons living animals, which they dismembered, and then distributed at cross-roads to a certain evil spirit of low rank, named the Son of Art.
3. They sought by their sorcery advice and responses from demons.
4. In their nightly meetings they blasphemously imitated the power of the Church by fulminating sentence of excommunication, with lighted candles, even against their own husbands, from the sole of their foot to the crown of their head, naming each part expressly, and then concluded by extinguishing the candles and by crying *Fi! Fi! Fi! Amen.*
5. In order to arouse feelings of love or hatred, or to inflict death or disease on the bodies of the faithful, they made use of powders, unguents, ointments, and candles of fat, which were compounded as follows. They took the entrails of cocks sacrificed to demons, certain horrible worms, various unspecified herbs, dead men's nails,

the hair, brains, and shreds of the cerements of boys who were buried unbaptized, with other abominations, all of which they cooked, with various incantations, over a fire of oak-logs in a vessel made out of the skull of a decapitated thief.

6. The children of Dame Alice's four husbands accused her before the Bishop of having killed their fathers by sorcery, and of having brought on them such stolidity of their senses that they bequeathed all their wealth to her and her favourite son, William Outlawe, to the impoverishment of the other children. They also stated that her present husband, Sir John le Poer, had been reduced to such a condition by sorcery and the use of powders that he had become terribly emaciated, his nails had dropped off, and there was no hair left on his body. No doubt he would have died had he not been warned by a maid-servant of what was happening, in consequence of which be had forcibly possessed himself of his wife's keys, and had opened some chests in which be found a sackful of horrible and detestable things which he transmitted to the bishop by the hands of two priests.

7. The said dame had a certain demon, an incubus, named Son of Art, or Robin son of Art, who had carnal knowledge of her, and from whom she admitted that she had received all her wealth. This incubus made its appearance under various forms, sometimes as a cat, or as a hairy black dog, or in the likeness of a negro (Æthiops), accompanied by two others who were larger and taller than he, and of whom one carried an iron rod.

According to another source the sacrifice to the evil spirit is said to have consisted of nine red cocks, and nine peacocks' eyes. Dame Alice was also accused of having "swept the streets of Kilkenny betweene compleine and twilight, raking all the filth towards the doores of hir sonne William Outlawe, murmuring secretly with hir selfe these words:

> "To the house of William my sonne
> Hie all the wealth of Kilkennie towne."

On ascertaining the above the Bishop wrote to the Chancellor of Ireland, Roger Outlawe, who was also Prior of the Preceptory of Kilmainham, for the arrest of these persons. Upon this William Outlawe formed a strong party to oppose the Bishop's demands, amongst which were the Chancellor, his near relative, and Sir Arnold le Poer, the Seneschal of Kilkenny, who was probably akin to Dame Alice's fourth husband. The Chancellor in reply wrote to the Bishop stating that a warrant for arrest could not be obtained until a public process of excommunication had been in force for forty days, while Sir Arnold also wrote requesting him to withdraw the case, or else to ignore it. Finding such obstacles placed in his way the Bishop took the matter into his own hands, and cited the Dame, who was then in her son's house in Kilkenny, to appear before him. As might be expected, she ignored the citation, and fled immediately.

Foiled in this, he cited her son William for heresy. Upon this Sir Arnold came with William to the Priory of Kells, where De Ledrede was holding a visitation, and besought him not to proceed further in the matter. Finding entreaty useless he had recourse to threats, which he speedily put into execution. As the Bishop was going forth on the following day to continue his visitation he was met on the confines of the town of Kells by Stephen le Poer, bailiff of the cantred of Overk, and a posse of armed men, by whom he was arrested under orders from Sir Arnold, and lodged the same day in Kilkenny jail. This naturally caused tremendous excitement in the city. The place became *ipso facto* subject to an interdict; the Bishop desired the Sacrament, and it was brought to him in solemn procession by the Dean and Chapter. All the clergy, both secular and religious, flocked from every side to the prison to offer their consolation to the captive, and their feelings were roused to the highest pitch by the preaching of a Dominican, who took as his text, *Blessed are they which are persecuted*, &c. Seeing this, William Outlawe nervously informed Sir Arnold of it, who thereupon decided to keep the Bishop in closer restraint, but subsequently changed his mind, and allowed him to have companions with him day and night, and also granted free admission to all his friends and servants.

After De Ledrede had been detained in prison for seventeen days, and Sir Arnold having thereby attained his end, viz. that the day on which William Outlawe was cited to appear should in the meantime pass by, he sent by the hands of his uncle the Bishop of Leighlin (Miler le Poer), and the sheriff of Kilkenny a mandate to the constable of the prison to liberate the Bishop. The latter refused to sneak out like a released felon, but assumed his pontificals, and, accompanied by all the clergy and a throng of people, made his way solemnly to S. Canice's Cathedral, where he gave thanks to God. With a pertinacity we cannot but admire he again cited William Outlawe by public proclamation to appear before him, but before the day arrived the Bishop was himself cited to answer in Dublin for having placed an interdict on his diocese. He excused himself from attending on the plea that the road thither passed through the lands of Sir Arnold, and that in consequence his life would be in danger.

De Ledrede had been arrested by Le Poer's orders in Lent, in the year 1324. On Monday following the octave of Easter the Seneschal held his court in Kilkenny, to which entrance was denied the Bishop; but the latter, fully robed, and carrying the Sacrament in a golden vase, made his way into the court-room, and "ascending the tribunal, and reverently elevating the Body of Christ, sought from the Seneschal, Justiciary, and Bailiffs that a hearing should be granted to him." The scene between the two was extraordinary; it is too lengthy to insert, and does not bear to be condensed—suffice it to say that the Seneschal alluded to the Bishop as "that vile, rustic, interloping monk (trutannus), with his dirt (hordys) which he is carrying in his hands," and refused to hear his arguments, or to afford him any assistance.

Though we have lost sight for a while of Dame Alice, yet she seems to have been eagerly watching the trend of events, for now we find her having the Bishop summoned to Dublin to answer for having excommunicated her, uncited, unadmonished, and unconvicted of the crime of sorcery. He attended accordingly, and found the King's and the Archbishop's courts against him to a man, but the upshot of the matter was that the Bishop won the day; Sir Arnold was humbled, and sought his pardon for the wrongs he had done him. This was granted, and in the presence of the council and the assembled prelates they mutually gave each other the kiss of peace.

Affairs having come to such a satisfactory conclusion the Bishop had leisure to turn his attention to the business that had unavoidably been laid aside for some little time. He directed letters patent, praying the Chancellor to seize the said Alice Kyteler, and also directed the Vicar-General of the Archbishop of Dublin to cite her to respond on a certain day in Kilkenny before the Bishop. But the bird escaped again out of the hand of the fowler. Dame Alice fled a second time, on this occasion from Dublin, where she had been living, and (it is said) made her way to England, where she spent the remainder of her days unmolested. Several of her confederates were subsequently arrested, some of them being apparently in a very humble condition of life, and were committed to prison. Their names were: Robert of Bristol, a clerk, John Galrussyn, Ellen Galrussyn, Syssok Galrussyn, William Payn de Boly, Petronilla of Meath, her daughter Sarah, [1] Alice the wife of Henry Faber, Annota Lange, and Eva de Brownestown. When the Bishop arrived in Kilkenny from Dublin he went direct to the prison, and interviewed the unfortunates mentioned above. They all immediately confessed to the charges laid against them, and even went to the length of admitting other crimes of which no mention had been made; but, according to them, Dame Alice was the mother and mistress of them all. Upon this the Bishop wrote letters on the 6th of June to the Chancellor, and to the Treasurer, Walter de Islep, requesting them to order the Sheriff to attach the bodies of these people and put them in safe keeping. But a warrant was refused, owing to the fact that William Outlawe was a relation of the one and a close friend of the other; so at length the Bishop obtained it through the Justiciary, who also consented to deal with the case when he came to Kilkenny.

Before his arrival the Bishop summoned William Outlawe to answer in S. Mary's Church. The latter appeared before him, accompanied by a band of men armed to the teeth; but in no way overawed by this show of force, De Ledrede formally accused him of heresy, of favouring, receiving, and defending heretics, as well as of usury, perjury, adultery, clericide, and excommunications—in all thirty-four items were brought forward against him, and he was permitted to respond on the arrival of the Justiciary. When the latter reached Kilkenny, accompanied by the Chancellor, the Treasurer, and the King's Council, the Bishop in their presence recited the charges against Dame Alice, and with the common consent of the lawyers present declared her to be a sorceress, magician, and heretic, and demanded that she should be handed over to the secular arm and have her goods and chattels confiscated as well. judging from Friar Clyn's note this took place on the 2nd of July. On the same day the Bishop caused a great fire to be lit in the middle of the town in which he burnt the sackful of magical stock-in-trade, consisting of powders, ointments, human nails, hair, herbs, worms, and other abominations, which the reader will remember he had received from Sir John le Poer at an early stage in the proceedings.

Further trouble arose with William Outlawe, who was backed by the Chancellor and Treasurer, but the Bishop finally succeeded in beating him, and compelled him to submit on his bended knees. By way of penance he was ordered to hear at least three masses every day for the space of a year, to feed a certain number of poor people, and to cover with lead the chancel of S. Canice's Cathedral from the belfry eastward, as well as the Chapel of the Blessed Virgin. He thankfully agreed to do this, but subsequently refused to fulfil his obligations, and was thereupon cast into prison.

What was the fate of Dame Alice's accomplices, whose names we have given above, is not specifically recorded, except in one particular instance. One of them, Petronilla of Meath, was made the scapegoat for her mistress. The Bishop had her flogged six times, and under the repeated application of this form of torture she made the required confession of magical practices. She admitted the denial of her faith and the sacrificing to Robert, son of Art, and as well that she had caused certain women of her acquaintance to appear as if they had goats' horns, She also confessed that at the suggestion of Dame Alice she had frequently consulted demons and received responses from them, and that she had acted as a "medium" (mediatrix) between her and the said Robert. She declared that although she herself was mistress of the Black Art, yet she was as nothing in comparison with the Dame from whom she had learnt all her knowledge, and that there was no one in the world more skilful than she. She also stated that William Outlawe deserved death as much as she, for he was privy to their sorceries, and for a year and a day had worn the devil's girdle [2] round his body. When rifling Dame Alice's house there was found "a wafer of sacramental bread, having the devil's name stamped thereon instead of Jesus Christ, and a pipe of ointment wherewith she greased a staffe, upon which she ambled and galloped through thicke and thin, when and in what manner she listed." Petronilla was accordingly condemned to be burnt alive, and the execution of this sentence took place with all due solemnity in Kilkenny on 3rd November 1324, which according to Clyn fell on a Sunday. This was the first instance of the punishment of death by fire being inflicted in Ireland for heresy.

Whether or not Petronilla's fellow-prisoners were punished is not clear, but the words of the anonymous narrator show us that the burning of that unfortunate wretch was rather the beginning than the end of persecution—that in fact numerous other suspected persons were followed up, some of whom shared her terrible fate, while to others milder forms of punishment were meted out, no doubt in proportion to their guilt. He says: "With regard to the other heretics and sorcerers who belonged to the pestilential society of Robin, son of Art, the order of law being pre, served, some of them were publicly burnt to death; others, confessing their crimes in the presence of all the people, in an upper garment, are marked back and front with a cross after they had abjured their heresy, as is the custom; others were solemnly whipped through the town and the market-place; others were banished from the city and diocese; others who evaded the jurisdiction of the Church were excommunicated; while others again fled in fear and were never heard of after. And thus, by the authority of Holy Mother Church, and by the special grace of God, that most foul brood was scattered and destroyed."

Sir Arnold le Poer, who had taken such a prominent part in the affair, was next attacked. The Bishop accused him of heresy, had him excommunicated, and committed prisoner to Dublin Castle. His innocency was believed in by most people, and Roger Outlawe, Prior of Kilmainham, who also figures in our story, and who was appointed Justiciary of Ireland in 1328, showed him some kindness, and treated him with humanity. This so enraged the Bishop that he actually accused the Justiciary of heresy. A select committee of clerics vindicated the orthodoxy of the latter, upon which he prepared a sumptuous banquet for his defenders. Le Poer died in prison the same year, 1331, before the matter was finally settled, and as he was under ban of excommunication his body lay unburied for a long period.

But ultimately the tables were turned with a vengeance. De Ledrede was himself accused of heresy by his Metropolitan, Alexander de Bicknor, upon which he appealed to the Holy See, and set out in person for Avignon. He endured a long exile from his diocese, suffered much hardship, and had his temporalities seized by the Crown as well. In 1339 he recovered the royal favour, but ten years later further accusations were brought to the king against him, in consequence of which the temporalities were a second time taken up, and other severe measures were threatened.

However, by 1356 the storm had blown over; he terminated a lengthy and disturbed episcopate in 1360, and was buried in the chancel of S. Canice's on the north side of the high altar. A recumbent effigy under an ogee-headed canopy is supposed to mark the last resting-place of this turbulent prelate.

In the foregoing pages we have only given the barest outline of the story, except that the portions relative to the practice of sorcery have been fully dealt with as pertinent to the purpose of this book, as well as on account of the importance of the case in the annals of Irish witchcraft. The story of Dame Alice Kyteler and Bishop de Ledrede occupies forty pages of the Camden Society's publications, while additional illustrative matter can be obtained from external sources; indeed, if all the scattered material were gathered together and carefully sifted it would be sufficient to make a short but interesting biography of that prelate, and would throw considerable light on the relations between Church and State in Ireland in the fourteenth century. With regard to the tale it is difficult to know what view should be taken of it. Possibly Dame Alice and her associates actually tried to practise magical arts, and if so, considering the period at which it occurred, we certainly cannot blame the Bishop for taking the steps he did. On the other hand, to judge from the analogy of Continental witchcraft, it is to be feared that De Ledrede was to some extent swayed by such baser motives as greed of gain and desire for revenge. He also seems to have been tyrannical, overbearing, and dictatorial; according to him the attitude adopted by the Church should never be questioned by the State, but this view was not shared by his opponents. Though our sympathies do not lie altogether with him, yet to give him his due it must be said that he was as ready to be persecuted as to persecute; he did not hesitate to face an opposition which consisted of some of the highest in the land, nor did fear of attack or imprisonment (which he actually suffered) avail to turn him aside from following the course he had mapped out for himself.

It should be noticed that the appointment of De Ledrede to the See of Ossory almost synchronised with the elevation of John XXII to the Papacy. The attitude of that Pope towards magical arts was no uncertain one. He believed himself to be surrounded by enemies who were ever making attempts on his life by modelling images of him in wax, to be subsequently thrust through with pins and melted, no doubt; or by sending him a devil enclosed in a ring, or in various other ways. Consequently in several Bulls he anathematised sorcerers, denounced their ill-deeds, excited the inquisitors against them, and so gave ecclesiastical authorisation to the reality of the belief in magical forces. Indeed, the general expressions used in the Bull *Super illius specula* might be applied to the actions of Dame Alice and her party. He says of certain persons that "they sacrifice to demons and adore them. making or causing to be made images, rings, &c., with which they draw the evil spirits by their magical art, obtain responses from them, and demand their help in performing their evil designs." [3]

Heresy and sorcery were now identified, and the punishment for the former was the same as that for the latter, viz. burning at the stake and confiscation of property. The attitude of this Pontiff evidently found a sympathiser in Bishop de Ledrede, who deemed it necessary to follow the example set by the Head of the Church, with what results we have already shown: thus we find in Ireland a ripple of the wave that swept over Europe at this period.

It is very probable, too, that there were many underlying local causes of which we can know little or nothing; the discontent and anger of the disinherited children at the loss of the wealth of which Dame Alice had bereft them by her exercise of "undue influence" over her husbands, family quarrels, private hatreds, and possibly national jealousy helped to bring about one of the strangest series of events in the chequered history of Ireland.

Footnotes

1. Elsewhere given as Basilia.
2. Magical girdles were used for various purposes. Bosc in his *Glossaire* will have them to be the origin of the magnetic belts, &c. that are so freely advertised at the present day.
3. Français, *op. cit.*

CHAPTER III

A.D. 1223-1583

THE KYTELER CASE AND ITS SURROUNDINGS OF SORCERY AND HERESY—MICHAEL SCOT—THE FOURTH EARL OF DESMOND—JAMES I AND THE IRISH PROPHETESS—A SORCERY ACCUSATION OF 1447—WITCHCRAFT TRIALS IN THE SIXTEENTH CENTURY—STATUTES DEALING WITH THE SUBJECT—EYE-BITERS—THE ENCHANTED EARL OF DESMOND

IN one respect the case of Dame Alice Kyteler stands alone in the history of magical dealings in Ireland prior to the seventeenth century. We have of the entire proceedings an invaluable and contemporary account, or at latest one compiled within a very few years after the death of Petronilla of Meath; while the excitement produced by the affair is shown by the more or less lengthy allusions to it in early writings, such as *The Book of Howth* (Carew MSS.), the Annals by Friar Clyn, the Chartularies of S. Mary's Abbey (vol. ii.), &c. It is also rendered more valuable by the fact that those who are best qualified to give their opinion on the matter have assured the writer that to the best of their belief no entries with respect to trials for sorcery or witchcraft can be found in the various old Rolls preserved in the Dublin Record Office.

But when the story is considered with reference to the following facts it takes on a different signification. On the 29th of September 1317 (Wright says 1320), Bishop de Ledrede held his first Synod, at which several canons were passed, one of which seems in some degree introductory to the events detailed in the preceding chapter. In it he speaks of "a certain new and pestilential sect in our parts, differing from all the faithful in the world, filled with a devilish spirit, more inhuman than heathens or Jews, who pursue the priests and bishops of the Most High God equally in life and death, by spoiling and rending the patrimony of Christ in the diocese of Ossory, and who utter grievous threats against the bishops and their ministers exercising ecclesiastical jurisdiction, and (by various means) attempt to hinder the correction of sins and the salvation of souls, in contempt of God and the Church." [1] From this it would seem that heresy and unorthodoxy had already made its appearance in the diocese. In 1324 the Kyteler case occurred, one of the participants being burnt at the stake, while other incriminated persons were subsequently followed up, some of whom shared the fate of Petronilla. In 1327 Adam *Dubh*, of the Leinster tribe of O'Toole, was burnt alive on College Green for denying the doctrines of the Incarnation and the Holy Trinity, as well as for rejecting the authority of the Holy See. [2] In 1335 Pope Benedict XII wrote a letter to King Edward III, in which occurs the following passage: "It has come to our knowledge that while our venerable brother, Richard, Bishop of Ossory, was visiting his diocese, there appeared in the midst of his catholic people men who were heretics together with their abettors, some of whom asserted that Jesus Christ was a mere man and a sinner, and was justly crucified for His own sins; others after having done homage and offered sacrifice to demons, thought otherwise of the sacrament of the Body of Christ than the Catholic Church teaches, saying that the same venerable sacrament is by no means to be worshipped; and also asserting that they are not bound to obey or believe the decrees, decretals, and apostolic mandates; in the meantime, consulting demons according to the rites of those sects among the Gentiles and Pagans, they despise the sacraments of the Catholic Church, and draw the faithful of Christ after them by their superstitions." As no Inquisitors of heresy have been appointed in Ireland, he begs the King to give prompt assistance to the Bishop and other Prelates in their efforts to punish the aforesaid heretics. [3] If the above refer to the Kyteler case it came rather late in the day; but it is quite possible, in view of the closing words of the anonymous narrator, that it has reference rather to the following up of the dame's associates, a process that must have involved a good deal of time and trouble, and in which no doubt many unhappy creatures were implicated. Again, in 1353, two men were tried at Bunratty in co. Clare by Roger Cradok, Bishop of Waterford, for holding heretical opinions (or for offering contumely to the Blessed Virgin), and were sentenced to be burnt. [4] The above are almost the only (if not the only) instances known of the punishment of death by fire being inflicted in Ireland for heresy.

From a consideration of the facts here enumerated it would seem as if a considerable portion of Ireland had been invaded by a wave of heresy in the first half of the fourteenth century, and that this manifested itself under a twofold form—first, in a denial of the cardinal doctrines of the Church and a consequent revolt against her jurisdiction'; and secondly, in the use of magical arts, incantations, charms, familiar spirits, *et hoc genus omne*. In this movement the Kyteler case was only an episode, though obviously the most prominent one; while its importance was considerably enhanced, if not exaggerated out of all due proportion, by the aggressive attitude adopted by Bishop de Ledrede against the lady and her companions, as well as by his struggles with Outlawe and Le Poer, and their powerful backers, the Chancellor and Treasurer of Ireland. The anonymous writer, who was plainly a cleric, and a partisan of the Bishop's, seems to have compiled his narration not so much on account of the incident of sorcery as to show the courage and perseverance of De Ledrede, and as well to make manifest the fact that the Church should dictate to the State, not the State to the Church. It appears quite possible, too, that other separate cases of sorcery occurred in Ireland at this period, though they had no historian to immortalise them, and no doubt in any event would have faded into insignificance in comparison with the doings of Dame Kyteler and her "infernal crew."

From this on we shall endeavour to deal with the subject as far as possible in chronological order. It is perhaps not generally known that at one time an Irish See narrowly escaped (to its misfortune, be it said) having a magician as its Chief Shepherd. In 1223 the Archbishopric of Cashel became vacant, upon which the Capitular Body elected as their Archbishop the then Bishop of Cork, to whom the temporalities were restored in the following year. But some little time prior to this the Pope had set aside the election and "provided" a nominee of his own, one Master M. Scot, to fill the vacancy: he however declined the proffered dignity on the ground that he was ignorant of the Irish language. This papal candidate was none other than the famous Michael Scot, reputed a wizard of such potency that—

> "When in Salamanca's cave
> Him listed his magic wand to wave
> The bells would ring in Notre Dame."

Scot had studied successively at Oxford and Paris (where he acquired the title of "mathematicus"); he then passed to Bologna, thence to Palermo, and subsequently continued his studies at Toledo. His refusal of the See of Cashel was an intellectual loss to the Irish Church, for, he was so widely renowned for his varied and extensive learning that he was credited with supernatural powers; a number of legends grew up around his name which hid his real merit, and transformed the man of science into a magician. In the Border country traditions of his magical power are common. Boccaccio alludes to "a great master in necromancy, called Michael Scot," while Dante places him in the eighth circle of Hell.

The next, who is so slender in the Ranks,
Was Michael Scot, who of a verity
Of magical illusions knew the game." [5]

Another man to whom magical powers were attributed solely on account of his learning was Gerald, the fourth Earl of Desmond, [6] styled the Poet, who died rather mysteriously in 1398. The Four Masters in their Annals describe him as "a nobleman of wonderful bounty, mirth, cheerfulness of conversation, charitable in his deeds, easy of access, a witty and ingenious composer of Irish poetry, a learned and profound chronicler." No legends are extant of his magical deeds.

King James I of Scotland, whose severities against his nobles had aroused their bitter resentment, was barbarously assassinated at p. 54}

Perth in 1437 by some of their supporters, who were aided and abetted by the aged Duke of Atholl. From a contemporary account of this we learn that the monarch's fate was predicted to him by an Irish prophetess or witch; had he given ear to her message he might have escaped with his life. We modernise the somewhat difficult spelling, but retain the quaint language of the original. "The king, suddenly advised, made a solemn feast of the Christmas at Perth, which is clept Saint John's Town, which is from Edinburgh on the other side of the Scottish sea, the which is vulgarly clept the water of Lethe. In the midst of the way there arose a woman of Ireland, that clept herself as a soothsayer. The which anon as she saw the king she cried with loud voice, saying thus: 'My lord king, and you pass this water you shall never turn again alive.' The king hearing this was astonied of her words; for but a little before he had read in a prophecy that in the self same year the king of Scots should be slain: and therewithal the king, as he rode, cleped to him one of his knights, and gave him in commandment to turn again to speak with that woman, and ask of her what she would, and what thing she meant with her loud crying. And she began, and told him as ye have heard of the King of Scots if he passed that water. As now the king asked her, how she knew that. And she said, that

Huthart told her so. 'Sire,' quoth he, 'men may "calant" ye take no heed of yon woman's words, for she is but a drunken fool, and wot not what she saith'; and so with his folk passed the water clept the Scottish sea, towards Saint John's town." The narrator states some dreams ominous of James's murder, and afterwards proceeds thus: "Both afore supper, and long after into quarter of the night, in the which the Earl of Atholl (Athetelles) and Robert Steward were about the king, where they were occupied at the playing of the chess, at the tables, in reading of romances, in singing and piping, in harping, and in other honest solaces of great pleasance and disport. Therewith came the said woman of Ireland, that clept herself a divineress, and entered the king's court, till that she came straight to the king's chamber-door, where she stood, and abode because that it was shut. And fast she knocked, till at the last the usher opened the door, marvelling of that woman's being there that time of night, and asking her what she would. 'Let me in, sir,' quoth she, 'for I have somewhat to say, and to tell unto the king; for I am the same woman that not long ago desired to have spoken with him at the Leith, when he should pass the Scottish sea.' The usher went in and told him of this woman. 'Yea,' quoth the king, 'let her come tomorrow'; because that he was occupied with such disports at that time him let not to hear her as then. The usher came again to the chamber-door to the said woman, and there he told her that the king was busy in playing, and bid her come soon again upon the morrow. 'Well,' said the woman, 'it shall repent you all that ye will not let me speak now with the king.' Thereat the usher laughed, and held her but a fool, charging her to go her way, and therewithal she went thence." Her informant "Huthart" was evidently a familiar spirit who was in attendance on her. [7]

Considering the barrenness of Irish records on the subject of sorcery and witchcraft it affords us no small satisfaction to find the following statement in the Statute Rolls of the Parliament [8] for the year 1447. It consists of a most indignantly-worded remonstrance from the Lords and Commons, which was drawn forth by the fact that some highly-placed personage had been accused of practising sorcery with the intent to do grievous harm to his enemy. When making it the remonstrants appear to have forgotten, or perhaps, like Members of Parliament in other ages, found it convenient to forget for the nonce the Kyteler incident of the previous century. Of the particular case here alluded to unfortunately no details are given, nor is any clue for obtaining them afforded us. The remonstrance runs as follows: "Also at the prayer of John, Archbishop of Armagh (and others). That whereas by the subtle malice and malicious suits of certain persons slandering a man of rank this land was entirely slandered, and still is in such slanderous matters as never were known in this land before, as in ruining or destroying any man by sorcery or necromancy., the which they think and believe impossible to be performed in art—It is ordained and agreed by authority of this present parliament, with the entire assent of the lords spiritual and temporal and commons of said parliament, that our lord the king be certified of the truth in this matter, in avoidance of the slander of this land in common, asserting that no such art was attempted at any time in this land, known or rumoured among the people, nor any opinion had or entertained of the same by the lay men in this land until now." It seems likely that the accusation was prompted by personal enmity, and was groundless in fact; but the annals of witchcraft show that such an indictment could prove a most terrible weapon in the hands of unscrupulous persons. With respect to the above we learn that Ireland was coming into line with England, for in the latter country during the fifteenth century charges of sorcery were frequently raised against persons of eminence by their political adversaries. One of the most celebrated cases of the kind occurred only six years prior to the above, in 1441, that of the Duchess of Gloucester in the reign of Henry VI.

Nothing further on the subject is recorded until the year 1544, under which date we find the following entry in the table of the red council book of Ireland:

"A letter to Charles FitzArthur for sendinge a witch to the Lord Deputie to be examined."

This note is a most tantalising one. The red council book has been lost, but a succinct "table" of its contents, from which the above has been extracted, and which was apparently compiled by Sir William Usher, has been preserved in Add. MSS. 1792, and published in Hist. MSS. Comm. 15th Report, appendix, part 3, but an examination of the original MS. reveals nothing in addition to the above passage; so, until the lost book is discovered, we must remain in ignorance with respect to the doings of this particular witch.

The next notice of witchcraft in Ireland occurs in the year 1578, when a witch-trial took place at Kilkenny, though here again, unfortunately, no details have been preserved.

In the November of that year sessions were held there by the Lord Justice Drury and Sir Henry Fitton, who, in their letter to the Privy Council on the 20th of the same month, inform that Body that upon arriving at the town "the jail being full we caused sessions immediately to be held. Thirty-six persons were executed, amongst whom were some good ones, *a blackamoor and two witches* by natural law, for that we find no law to try them by in this realm." [9] It is easy to see why the witches were put to death, but the reason for the negro's execution is not so obvious. It can hardly have been for the colour of his skin, although no doubt a black man was as much a *rara avis* in the town of Kilkenny as a black swan. Had the words been written at the time the unfortunate negro might well have exclaimed, though in vain, to his judges:

"Mislike me not for my complexion—
The shadowed livery of the burning sun."

Or could it have been that he was the unhappy victim of a false etymology! For in old writers the word "necromancy" is spelt "nigromancy," as if divination was practised through the medium of *negroes* instead of *dead persons*; indeed in an old vocabulary of 1475 "Nigromantia" is defined as "divinatio facta *per nigros*." He may therefore have been suspected of complicity with the two witches.

As yet the "natural law" held sway in Ireland, but very soon this country was to be fully equipped with a Statute all to itself. Two Statutes against witchcraft had already been passed in England, one in 1541, which was repealed six years later, and a second in 1562. Partly no doubt on account of the Kilkenny case of 1578, and partly to place Ireland on the same footing as England, a Statute was passed by the Irish Parliament in 1586. Shorn of much legal verbiage the principal points of it may be gathered from the following extracts:

"Where at this present there is no ordinarie ne condigne punishment provided against the practices of the wicked offences of conjurations, and of invocations of evill spirites, and of sorceries, enchauntments, charms, and witchcrafts, whereby manie fantasticall and devilish persons have devised and practised invocations and conjurations of evill and wicked spirites, and have used and practised witchcrafts, enchauntments, charms, and sorceries, to the destruction of the persons and goods of their neighbours, and other subjects of this realm, and for other lewde and evill intents and purposes, contrary to the laws of Almighty God, to the peril of their owne soules, and to the great infamie and disquietnesse of this realm. For reformation thereof, be it enacted by the Queen's Majestie, with the assent of the lords spirituall and temporall and the commons in this present Parliament assembled.

"1. That if any person or persons after the end of three months next, and immediately after the end of the last session of this present parliament, shall use, practise, or exercise any witchcraft, enchauntment, charme, or sorcery, whereby any person shall happen to be killed or destroied, that then as well any such offender or offenders in invocations and conjurations, as is aforesaid, their aydors or councelors ... being of the said offences lawfully convicted and attainted, shall suffer paines of death as a felon or felons, and shall lose the privilege and benefit of clergie and sanctuarie; saving to the widow of such person her title of dower, and also the heires and successors of such a person all rights, titles, &c., as though no such attaynder had been made.

"2. If any persons (after the above period) shall use, practise, or exercise any witchcraft, enchauntment, charme, or sorcery, whereby any person or persons shall happen to be wasted, consumed, or lamed, in his or their bodie or member, or whereby any goods or cattels of any such person shall be destroyed, wasted, or impaired, then every such offender shall for the first offence suffer imprisonment by the space of one yeare without bayle or maineprise, and once in every quarter of the said yeare, shall in some market towne, upon the market day, or at such time as any faire shall be kept there, stand openlie in the pillorie for the space of sixe houres, and shall there openly confesse his or theire errour and offence, and for the second offence shall suffer death as a felon, saving, &c. (as in clause 1).

"3. Provided always, that if the offender in any of the cases aforesaid, for which the paines of death shall ensue, shall happen to be a peer of this realm: then his triall therein to be had by his peers, as is used in cases of felony and treason, and not otherwise.

"4. And further, to the intent that all manner of practice, use, or exercise of witchcraft, enchauntment, charme, or sorcery, should be from henceforth utterly avoide, abolished. and taken away; be it enacted by the authority of this present Parliament that if any person or persons . . . shall take upon them by witchcraft, &c., to tell or declare in what place any treasure of gold or silver shall or might be found or had in the earth or other secret Places, or where goods or things lost or stollen should be found or become, or shall use or practice any sorcery, &c., to the intent to provoke any person to unlawful love (for the first offence to be punished as in clause 2), but if convicted a second time shall forfeit unto the Queen's Majesty all his goods and chattels, and suffer imprisonment during life."

On the whole, considering the temper of the time, this Statute was exceedingly mild. It made no provision whatsoever for the use of torture to extract evidence, nor indeed did it offer any particular encouragement to the witch hunter, while the manner of inflicting the death penalty was precisely that for felony, viz. hanging, drawing, and quartering for men, and burning (preceded by strangulation) for women—sufficiently unpleasant, no doubt, but far more merciful than burning alive at the stake.

In some way Ireland was fortunate enough to escape the notice of that keen witch hunter, King James I and VI; had it been otherwise we have little doubt but that this country would have contributed its share to the list of victims in that monarch's reign. The above was therefore the only Statute against witchcraft passed by the Irish Parliament; it is said that it was never repealed, and so no doubt is in force at the present day. Another Act of the Parliament of Ireland, passed in 1634, and designed to facilitate the administration of justice, makes mention of witchcraft, and it is there held to be one of the recognised methods by which one man could take the life of another.

"Forasmuch as the most necessary office and duty of law is to preserve and save the life of man, and condignly to punish such persons that unlawfully or wilfully murder, slay, or destroy men . . . and where it often happeneth that a man is feloniously strucken in one county, and dieth in another county, in which case it hath not been found by the laws of this realm that any sufficient indictment thereof can be taken in any of the said two counties . . . For redress and punishment of such offences . . . be it enacted . . . that where any person shall be traiterously or feloniously stricken, poysoned, or *bewitched* in one county (and die in another, or out of the kingdom, &c.), that an indictment thereof found by jurors in the county where the death shall happen, shall be as good and effectual in the law as if, &c. &c.)."

Before passing from the subject we may note a curious allusion to a mythical Act of Parliament which was intended to put a stop to a certain lucrative form of witchcraft. It is gravely stated by the writer of a little book entitled *Beware the Cat* [10] (and by Giraldus Cambrensis before him), that Irish witches could turn wisps of hay, straw, &c. into red-coloured pigs, which they dishonestly sold in the market, but which resumed their proper shape when crossing running water. To prevent this it is stated that the Irish Parliament passed an Act forbidding the purchase of red swine. We regret to say, however, that no such interesting Act is to be found in the Statute books.

The belief in the power of witches to inflict harm on the cattle of those whom they hated, of which we have given some modern illustrations in the concluding chapter, was to be found in Elizabethan times in this country. Indeed if we are to put credence in the following passage from Reginald Scot, quoted by Thomas Ady in his *Perfect Discovery of Witches* (London, 1661), a certain amount of witch persecution arose with reference to this point, possibly as a natural outcome of the Statute of 1586. "Master Scot in his Discovery telleth us, that our English people in Ireland, whose posterity were lately barbarously cut off, were much given to this Idolatry [belief in witches] in the Queen's time [Elizabeth], insomuch that there being a Disease amongst their Cattel that grew blinde, being a common Disease in that Country, they did commonly execute people for it, calling them *eye-biting* Witches."

From incidental notices in writers of the latter half of the sixteenth century it would seem at first sight as if witchcraft, as we are treating of it in this work, was very prevalent in Ireland at this period. Barnabe Rich says in his description of Ireland: "The Irish are wonderfully addicted to give credence to the prognostications of Soothsayers and Witches." Stanihurst writes that in his time (1547-1618) there were many sorcerers amongst the Irish. A note in Dr. Hanmer's Collection speaks of "Tyrone his witch the which he hanged." [11] But these statements seem rather to have reference to the point of view from which the English writers regarded the native bards, as well as the "wise women" who foretold the future; probably "Tyrone" put his "witch" to death, not through abhorrence of her unhallowed doings, but in a fit of passion because her interpretation of coming events, by which he may have allowed himself to be guided, turned out wrongly.

We have already alluded to Gerald, the fourth Earl of Desmond. His namesake, the sixteenth holder of the title, commonly known as the "Great Earl," who was betrayed and killed in 1583, has passed from the region of history to that of mythology, as he is credited with being the husband (or son) of a goddess. Not many miles from the city of Limerick is a lonely, picturesque lake, Lough Gur, which was included in his extensive possessions, and at the bottom of which he is supposed to lie enchanted. According to the legend [12] he was a very potent magician, and usually resided in a castle which was built on a small island in that lake. To this he brought his bride, a young and beautiful girl, whom he loved with a too fond love, for she succeeded in prevailing upon him to gratify her selfish desires, with fatal results. One day she presented herself in the chamber in which her husband exercised his forbidden art, and begged him to show her the wonders of his evil science. With the greatest reluctance he consented, but warned her that she must prepare herself to witness a series of most frightful phenomena, which, once commenced, could neither be abridged nor mitigated, while if she spoke a single word during the proceedings the castle and all it contained would sink to the bottom of the lake.

Urged on by curiosity she gave the required promise, and he commenced. Muttering a spell as he stood before her, feathers sprouted thickly over him, his face became contracted and hooked, a corpse-like smell filled the air, and winnowing the air with beats of its heavy wings a gigantic vulture rose in his stead, and swept round and round the room as if on the point of pouncing upon her. The lady controlled herself through this trial, and another began.

The bird alighted near the door, and in less than a minute changed, she saw not how, into a horribly deformed and dwarfish hag, who, with yellow skin hanging about her face, and cavernous eyes, swung herself on crutches towards the lady, her mouth foaming with fury, and her grimaces and contortions becoming more and more hideous every moment, till she rolled with a fearful yell on the floor in a horrible convulsion at the lady's feet, and then changed into a huge serpent, which came sweeping and arching towards her with crest erect and quivering tongue.

Suddenly, as it seemed on the point of darting at her, she saw her husband in its stead, standing pale before her, and with his finger on his lips enforcing the continued necessity of silence. He then placed himself at full length on the floor and began to stretch himself out, longer and longer, until his head nearly reached to one end of the vast room and his feet to the other. This utterly unnerved her. She gave a wild scream of horror, whereupon the castle and all in it sank to the bottom of the lake.

Once in seven years the great Earl rises, and rides by night on his white horse round Lough Gur. The steed is shod with silver shoes, and when these are worn out the spell that holds the Earl will be broken, and he will regain possession of his vast estates and semi-regal power. In the opening years of the nineteenth century there was living a man named Teigue O'Neill, who claimed to have seen him on the occasion of one of his septennial appearances under the following curious conditions. O'Neill was a blacksmith, and his forge: stood on the brow of a hill overlooking the lake, on a lonely part of the road to Cahirconlish. One night, when there was a bright moon, he was working very late and quite alone. In one of the pauses of his work he heard the ring of many hoofs ascending the steep road that passed his forge, and, standing in his doorway, he saw a gentleman on a white horse, who was dressed in a fashion the like of which he had never seen before. This man was accompanied by a mounted retinue, in similar dress. They seemed to be riding up the hill at a gallop, but the pace slackened as they drew near, and the rider of the white horse, who seemed from his haughty air to be a man of rank, drew bridle, and came to a halt before the smith's door. He did not speak, and all his train were silent, but he beckoned to the smith, and pointed down at one of the horse's hoofs. Teigue stooped and raised it, and held it just long enough to see that it was shod with a silver shoe, which in one place was worn as thin as a shilling. Instantly his situation was made apparent to him by this sign, and he recoiled with a terrified prayer. The lordly rider, with a look of pain and fury, struck at him suddenly with something that whistled in the air like a whip; an icy streak seemed to traverse his body, and at the same time he saw the whole cavalcade break into a gallop, and disappear down the hill. It is generally supposed that for the purpose of putting an end to his period of enchantment the Earl endeavours to lead someone on to first break the silence and speak to him; but what, in the event of his succeeding, would be the result, or would befall the person thus ensnared, no one knows.

In a letter [13] written in the year 1640, the Earl assumes a different appearance. We learn from it that as a countryman was on his way to the ancient and celebrated fair of Knockaney, situated a few miles from Lough Gur, he met "a gentleman standing in the waye, demanding if he would sell his horse. He answered, yea, for £5. The gentleman would give him but £4, 10 s., saying he would not get so much at the ffaire. The fellow went to the ffaire, could not get so much money, and found the gentleman on his return in the same place, who proffered the same money. The fellow accepting of it, the other bid him come in and receive his money. He carried him into a fine spacious castle, payed him his money every penny, and showed him the fairest black horse that ever was seene, and told him that that horse was the Earl of Desmond, and that he had three shoes alreadye, when he hath the fourthe shoe, which should be very shortlie, then should the Earl be as he was before, thus guarded with many armed men conveying him out of the gates. The fellow came home, but never was any castle in that place either before or since." The local variant of the legend states that the seller of the horse was a Clare man, and that he went home after having been paid in gold the full amount of a satisfactory bargain, but on the following morning found to his great mortification, that instead of the gold coins he had only a pocketful of ivy leaves. Readers of Victor Hugo's *Notre Dame* will recall the incident of the *écu*

49

that (apparently) was transformed by magic into a withered leaf. Similar tales of horse-dealing with mysterious strangers are told in Scotland in connection with the celebrated Thomas the Rhymer, of Erceldoune.

Footnotes

1. Carrigan, *History of the Diocese of Ossory*, i. p. 48.
2. Stokes, *Ireland and the Anglo-Norman Church*, p. 374.
3. Theiner, *Vet. Mon.*, p. 269.
4. Westropp, *Wars of Turlough* (Proc. R.I.A.), p. 161; Seymour, *Pre-Ref. Archbishops of Cashel*, 47.
5. *Dict. Nat. Biog.*, Seymour, *op. cit.*, p. 18.
6. O'Daly, *History of the Geraldines*.
7. Sharpe, *History of Witchcraft in Scotland*, p. 30.
8. Ed. H. F. Berry, D.Litt.
9. Carrigan, *op. cit.*, iii. p. 18.
10. Quoted in *Journal of Royal Society of Antiquaries*, 3rd series, vol. i. Français mentions a Swiss sorcerer, somewhat of a wag, who used to play the same trick on people.
11. *Ulster Journal of Archæology*, vol. iv. (for 1858).
12. *All the Year Round* (for April 1870).
13. Lenihan, *History of Limerick*, p. 147.

CHAPTER IV

A.D. 1606-1656

A CLERICAL WIZARD—WITCHCRAFT CURED BY A RELIC—RAISING THE DEVIL IN IRELAND—HOW HE WAS CHEATED BY A DOCTOR OF DIVINITY—STEWART AND THE FAIRIES—REV. ROBERT BLAIR AND THE MAN POSSESSED WITH A DEVIL—STRANGE OCCURRENCES NEAR LIMERICK—APPARITIONS OF MURDERED PEOPLE AT PORTADOWN—CHARMED LIVES-VISIONS AND PORTENTS—PETITION OF A BEWITCHED ANTRIM MAN IN ENGLAND—ARCHBISHOP USHER'S PROPHECIES—MR. BROWNE AND THE LOCKED CHEST

AN interesting trial of a clergyman for the practice of unhallowed arts took place early in 1606—interesting and valuable, if for no other reason than that it is the first instance of such a case being discovered in the Rolls at the Record Office (not counting those of the Parliament of 1447), though we hope that it will not prove to be a unique entry, but rather the earnest of others. Shorn of legal redundancies it runs as follows: "Inquiry taken before our lord the King at the King's Court the

Saturday next after the three weeks of Easter in the 6th year of James I by the oath of upright and lawful men of the County of Louth. Who say, that John Aston, late of Mellifont, Co. Louth, clerk, not having the fear of God before his eyes, but being wholly seduced by the devil, on December 1st at Mellifont aforesaid, and on divers other days and places, wickedly and feloniously used, practised, and exercised divers invocations and conjurings of wicked and lying spirits with the intent and purpose that he might find and recover a certain silver cup formerly taken away at Mellifont aforesaid, and also that he might understand where and in what region the most wicked traitor Hugh, Earl of Tyrone, then was, and what he was contriving against the said lord the King and the State of this kingdom of Ireland, and also that he might find out and obtain divers treasures of gold and silver concealed in the earth at Mellifont aforesaid and at Cashel in the county of the Cross of Tipperary, feloniously and against the peace of the said lord the King. It is to be known that the aforesaid John was taken, and being a prisoner in the Castle of the City of Dublin by warrant of the lord King was sent into England, therefore further proceedings shall cease." [1] His ultimate fate is not known; nor is it easy to see why punishment was not meted out to him in Ireland, as he had directly contravened section 4 of the Elizabethan Act. Possibly the case was unique, and so King James may have been anxious to examine in person such an interesting specimen. If so, heaven help the poor parson in the grip of such a witch hunter.

In the year 1609 there comes from the County of Tipperary a strange story of magical spells being counteracted by the application of a holy relic; this is preserved for us in that valuable monastic record, the *Triumphalia S. Crucis*. At Holy Cross Abbey, near Thurles, there was preserved for many years with the greatest veneration a supposed fragment of the True Cross, which attracted vast numbers of people, and by which it was said many wonderful miracles were worked. Amongst those that came thither in that year was "Anastasia Sobechan, an inhabitant of the district of Callan (co. Kilkenny), tortured by magical spells (veneficis incantationibus collisa), who at the Abbey, in presence of the Rev. Lord Abbot Bernard [Foulow], placed a girdle round her body that had touched the holy relic. Suddenly she vomited small pieces of cloth and wood, and for a whole month she spat out from her body such things. The said woman told this miracle to the Rev. Lord Abbot while she was healed by the virtue of the holy Cross. This be took care to set down in writing."

That most diligent gleaner of things strange and uncommon, Mr. Robert Law, to whom we are deeply indebted for much of the matter in this volume, informs us in his *Memorialls* that in the first half of the seventeenth century there was to be found in Ireland a celebrated Doctor of Divinity, in Holy Orders of the Episcopal Church, who possessed extreme adroitness in raising the Devil-a process that some would have us believe to be commonly practised in Ireland at the present day by persons who have no pretensions to a knowledge of the Black Art! Mr. Law also gives the *modus operandi* at full length. A servant-girl in the employment of Major-General Montgomerie at Irvine in Scotland was accused of having stolen some silver-work. "The lass being innocent takes it ill, and tells them, If she should raise the Devil she should know who took these things." Thereupon, in order to summon that Personage she went into a cellar, "takes the Bible with her, and draws a circle about her, and turns a riddle on end from south to north, or from the right to the left hand [*i.e.* contrary to the path of the sun in the heavens], having in her right hand nine feathers which she pulled out of the tail of a black cock, and having read the 51st [Psalm?] forwards, she reads backwards chapter ix., verse 19, of the Book of Revelation." Upon this the Devil appeared to her, and told her who was the guilty person. She then cast three of the feathers at him, and bade him return to the place from whence he came. This process she repeated three times, until she had gained all the information she desired; she then went upstairs and told her mistress, with the result that the goods were ultimately recovered. But escaping Scylla she fell into Charybdis; her uncanny practices came to the ears of the authorities, and she was apprehended. When in prison she confessed that she had learnt this particular branch of the Black Art in the house of Dr. Colville in Ireland, who habitually practised it.

That instructor of youth in such unchristian practices, the Rev. Alexander Colville, D.D., was ordained in 1622 and subsequently held the vicarage of Carnmoney, the prebend of Carncastle, and the Precentorship of Connor. He was possessed of considerable wealth, with which he purchased the Galgorm estate, on which he resided; this subsequently passed into the Mountcashel family through the marriage of his great granddaughter with Stephen Moore, first Baron Kilworth and Viscount Mountcashel. Where Dr. Colville got the money to purchase so large an estate no one could imagine, and Classon Porter in his useful pamphlet relates for us the manner in which popular rumour solved the problem. It was said that he had sold himself to the Devil, and that he had purchased the estate with the money his body and soul had realised. Scandal even went further still, and gave the exact terms which Dr. Colville had made with the Evil One. These were, that the Devil was at once to give the Doctor his hat full of gold, and that the latter was in return, at a distant but specified day, to deliver himself body and soul to the Devil. The appointed place of meeting was a lime-kiln; the Devil may have thought that this was a delicate compliment to him on account of the peculiarly *homelike* atmosphere of the spot, but the Doctor had different ideas. The Devil produced the gold, whereupon Dr. Colville produced a hat *with a wide slit in the crown*, which he boldly held over the empty kiln-pit, with the result that by the time the terms of the bargain were literally complied with, a very considerable amount of gold lay at the Doctor's disposal, which he prudently used to advance his worldly welfare.

So far, so good. But there are two sides to every question. Years rolled by, bringing ever nearer and nearer the time at which the account had to be settled, and at length the fatal day dawned. The Devil arrived to claim his victim, and found him sitting in his house reading his Bible by the light of a candle, whereupon he directed him to come along with him.

The Doctor begged that he might not be taken away until the candle, by which he was reading, was burned out. To this the Devil assented, whereupon Dr. Colville promptly extinguished the candle, and putting it between the leaves of the Bible locked it up in the chest where he kept his gold. The candle was thus deposited in a place of safety where there was no danger of any person coming across it, and thus of being the innocent cause of the Doctor's destruction. It is; even said that he gave orders that the candle should be put into his coffin and buried with him. So, we may presume, Dr. Colville evaded the payment of his debt. Our readers may perchance wonder why such stories as the above should have become connected with the reverend gentleman,. and an explanation is not hard to be found. Dr. Colville was a well-known divine, possessed of great wealth (inherited lawfully, we may presume), and enjoyed considerable influence in the country-side. At this time Ulster was overrun by triumphant Presbyterianism, which the Doctor, as a firm upholder of Episcopacy, opposed with all his might, and thereupon was spoken of with great acerbity by his opponents. It is not too uncharitable, therefore, to assume that these stories originated with some member of that body, who may well have believed that such had actually happened.

For the next instance of witchcraft and the supernatural in connection with Ireland we are compelled to go beyond the confines of our country. Though in this the connection with the Green Isle is slight, yet it is of interest as affording an example of that blending of fairy lore with sorcery which is not an uncommon feature of Scottish witchcraft-trials. In the year 1613 a woman named Margaret Barclay, of Irvine in Scotland, was accused of having caused her brother-in-law's ship to be cast away by magical spells. A certain strolling vagabond and juggler, John Stewart, was apprehended as her accomplice; be admitted (probably under torture) that Margaret had applied to him to teach her some magic arts in order that "she might get gear, kye's milk, love of man, her heart's desire on such persons as had done her wrong." Though he does not appear to have granted her request, yet he gave detailed information as to the manner in which he had gained the supernatural power and knowledge with which he was credited. "It being demanded of him by what means he professed himself to have knowledge of things to come, the said John confessed that the space of twenty-six years ago, he being travelling on All-Hallow Even night between the towns of Monygoif and Clary, in Galway, he met with the King of the Fairies and his company, and that the King gave him a stroke with a white rod over the forehead, which took from him the power of speech and the use of one eye, which he wanted for the space of three years. He declared that the use of speech and eyesight was restored to him by the King of Fairies and his company on a Hallowe'en night at the town of Dublin." At his subsequent meetings with the fairy band he was taught all his knowledge. The spot on which he was struck remained impervious to pain although a pin was thrust into it. The unfortunate wretch was cast into prison, and there committed suicide by hanging himself from the "cruik" of the door with his garter or bonnet-string, and so "ended his life miserably with the help of the devil his master." 2

A tale slightly resembling portion of the above comes from the north of Ireland a few years later. "It's storied, and the story is true," says Robert Law in his *Memorialls*, 3 "of a godly man in Ireland, who lying one day in the fields sleeping, he was struck with dumbness and deafness. The same man, during this condition he was in, could tell things, and had the knowledge of things in a strange way, which he had not before; and did, indeed, by signs make things known to others which they knew not. Afterwards he at length, prayer being made for him by others, came to the use of his tongue and ears; but when that knowledge of things he had in his deaf and dumb condition ceased, and when he was asked how he had the knowledge of these things he made signs of, he answered he had that knowledge when dumb, but how and after what manner he knew not, only he had the impression thereof in his spirit. This story was related by a godly minister, Mr. Robert Blair, to Mr. John Baird, who knew the truth of it."

The Rev. Robert Blair, M.A., was a celebrated man, if for no other reason than on account of his disputes with Dr. Echlin, Bishop of Down, or for his description of Oliver Cromwell as a *greeting* (*i.e.* weeping) devil. On the invitation of Lord Claneboy he arrived in Ireland in 1623, and in the same year was settled as (Presbyterian) parish minister at Bangor in Co. Down, with the consent of patron and people; he remained there until 1631, when he was suspended by Dr. Echlin, and was deposed and excommunicated in November, 1634. He has left a few writings behind him, and was grandfather of the poet Robert Blair, author of *The Grave*. [4]

During the years of his ministry at Bangor the following incident occurred to him, which he of course attributes to demonic possession, though homicidal mania resulting from intemperate habits would be nearer the truth. One day a rich man, the constable of the parish, called upon him in company with one of his tenants concerning the baptizing of the latter's child. "When I had spoken what I thought necessary, and was ready to turn into my house, the constable dismissing the other told me he had something to say to me in private. I looking upon him saw his eyes like the eyes of a cat in the night, did presently conceive that he had a mischief in his heart, yet I resolved not to refuse what he desired, but I keeped a watchful eye upon him, and stayed at some distance; and being near to the door of the church I went in, and invited him to follow me. As soon as he entered within the doors he fell atrembling, and I, awondering. His trembling continuing and growing without any speech, I approached to him, and invited him to a seat, w, herein he could hardly sit. The great trembling was like to throw him out of the seat. I laid my arm about him, and asked him what ailed him? But for a time he could speak none. At last his shaking ceased, and he began to speak, telling me, that for a long time the Devil had appeared to him; first at Glasgow he bought a horse from him, receiving a sixpence in earnest, and that in the end he offered to him a great purse full of sylver to be his, making no mention of the horse; he said that he blessed himself, and so the buyer with the sylver and gold that was poured out upon the table vanished. But some days thereafter he appeared to him at his own house, naming him by his name, and said to him, Ye are mine, for I *arled* you with a sixpence, which yet ye have. Then said he, I asked his name, and he answered, they call me *Nickel Downus* (I suppose that he repeated evil, that he should have said *Nihil Damus*). Being thus molested with these and many other apparitions of the Devil, he left Scotland; but being come to Ireland he did often likewise appear to him, and now of late he still commands me to kill and slay; and oftentimes, says he, my whinger hath been drawn and kept under my cloak to obey his commands, but still something holds my hand that I cannot strike. But then I asked him go whom he was bidden kill? He answered, any that comes in my way; but

'The better they be
The better service to me,
Or else I shall kill thee.'

When he uttered these words he fell again atrembling, and was stopped in his speaking, looking lamentably at me, designing me to be the person he aimed at; then he fell a crying and lamenting. I showed him the horribleness of his ignorance and drunkenness; he made many promises of reformation, which were not well keep'd; for within a fortnight he went to an alehouse to crave the price of his malt, and sitting there long at drink, as he was going homeward the Devil appeared to him, and challenged him for opening to me what had passed betwixt them secretly, and followed him to the house, pulling his cap off his head and his band from about his neck, saying to him, I On Hallow-night I shall have thee, soul and body, in despite of the minister and of all that he will do for thee.'"

In his choice of a date his Satanic Majesty showed his respect for popular superstitions. This attack of delirium tremens (though Mr. Blair would not have so explained it) had a most salutary effect; the constable was in such an abject state of terror lest the Devil should carry him off that he begged Mr. Blair to sit up with him all Hallow-night, which he did, spending the time very profitably in prayer and exhortation, which encouraged the man to defy Satan and all his works. The upshot of the matter was, that he became very charitable to the poor, and seems to have entirely renounced his intemperate habits. [5]

Rejecting the supernatural element in the above as being merely the fruits of a diseased mind, there is no reason to doubt the truth of the story. Mr. Blair also met with some strange cases of religious hysteria, which became manifest in outbursts of weeping and bodily convulsions, but which he attributed to the Devils "playing the ape, and counterfeiting the works of the Lord." He states that one Sunday, in the midst of public worship,

"one of my charge, being a dull and ignorant person, made a noise and stretching of her body. Incontinent I was assisted to rebuke that lying spirit that disturbed the worship of God, charging the same not to disturb the congregation; and through God's mercy we met with no more of that work." Thus modestly our writer sets down what happened in his *Autobiography*; but the account of the incident spread far and wide, and at length came to the ears of Archbishop Usher, who, on his next meeting with Mr. Blair, warmly congratulated him on the successful exorcism he had practised. [6]

If the period treated of in this chapter, viz. from the commencement of the seventeenth century to the Restoration of Charles II, be barren of witchcraft proper, it must at least be admitted that it is prodigal in regard to the marvellous under various shapes and forms, from which the hysterical state of the public mind can be fairly accurately gauged. The rebellion of 1641, and the Cromwellian confiscations, that troubled period when the country was torn by dissention, and ravaged by fire, sword, and pestilence, was aptly ushered in by a series of supernatural events which occurred in the county of Limerick. A letter dated the 13th August 1640, states that "for news we have the strangest that ever was heard of, there inchantments in the Lord of Castleconnell's Castle four miles from Lymerick, several sorts of noyse, sometymes of drums and trumpets, sometimes of other curious musique with heavenly voyces, then fearful screeches, and such outcries that the neighbours near cannot sleepe. Priests have adventured to be there, but have been cruelly beaten for their paynes, and carryed away they knew not how, some two miles and some four miles. Moreover were seen in the like manner, after they appear to the view of the neighbours, infinite number of armed men on foote as well as on horseback . . . One thing more [*i.e.* something supernatural] by Mrs. Mary Burke with twelve servants yes in the house, and never one hurt, onley they must dance with them every night; they say, Mrs. Mary come away, telling her she must be wyfe to the inchanted Earl of Desmond . . . Uppon a Mannour of my Lord Bishoppe of Lymerick, Loughill, hath been seen upon the hill by most of the inhabitants aboundance of armed men marching, and these seene many tymes—and when they come up to them they do not appeare. These things are very strange, if the cleargie and gentrie say true." [7]

During the rebellion an appalling massacre of Protestants took place at Portadown, when about a hundred persons, men, women, and children, were forced over the bridge into the river, and so drowned; the few that could swim, and so managed to reach the shore, were either knocked on the head by the insurgents when they landed, or else were shot. It is not a matter of surprise that this terrible incident gave rise to legends and stories in which anything strange or out of the common was magnified out of all proportion. According to one deponent there appeared one evening in the river "a vision or spirit assuming the shape of a woman, waist high, upright in the water, naked with [*illegible*] in her hand, her hair dishevelled, her eyes seeming to twinkle in her head, and her skin as white as snow; which spirit seeming to stand upright in the water often repeated the word *Revenge! Revenge! Revenge!*" Also Robert Maxwell, Archdeacon of Down, swore that the rebels declared to him, (and some deponents made similar statements) "that most of those that were thrown from that bridge were daily and nightly seen to walk upon the River, sometimes singing Psalms, sometimes brandishing of Swords, sometimes screeching in a most hideous and fearful manner." Both these occurrences are capable of a rational explanation. The supposed spectre was probably a poor, bereaved woman, demented by grief and terror, who stole out of her hiding-place at night to bewail the murder of her friends, while the weird cries arose from the half-starved dogs of the country-side, together with the wolves which abounded in Ireland at that period, quarrelling and fighting over the corpses. Granting the above, and bearing in mind the credulity of all classes of Society, it is not difficult to see how the tales originated; but to say that, because such obviously impossible statements occur in certain depositions, the latter are therefore worthless as a whole, is to wilfully misunderstand the popular mind of the seventeenth century.

We have the following on the testimony of the Rev. George Creighton, minister of Virginia, co. Cavan. He tells us that "divers women brought to his House a young woman, almost naked, to whom a Rogue came upon the way, these women being present, and required her to give him her mony, or else he would kill her, and so drew his sword; her answer was, You cannot kill me unless God give you leave, and His will be done. Thereupon the Rogue thrust three times at her naked body with his drawn sword, and never pierced her skin; whereat he being, as it seems, much confounded, went away and left her." A like story comes from the other side: "At the taking of the Newry a rebel being appointed to be shot upon the bridge, and stripped stark-naked, notwithstanding the musketeer stood within two yards of him, and shot him in the middle of the back, yet the bullet entered not, nor did him any more hurt than leave a little black spot behind it. This many hundreds were eye-witnesses of. Divers of the like have I confidently been assured of, who have been provided of diabolical charms." [8] Similar tales of persons bearing charmed lives could no doubt be culled from the records of every war that has been fought on this planet of ours since History began.

The ease with which the accidental or unusual was transformed into the miraculous at this period is shown by the following. A Dr. Tate and his wife and children were flying to Dublin from the insurgents. On their way they were wandering over commons covered with snow, without any food. The wife was carrying a sucking child, John, and having no milk to give it she was about to lay it down in despair, when suddenly "on the Brow of a Bank she found a Suck-bottle with sweet milk in it, no Footsteps appearing in the snow of any that should bring it thither, and far from any Habitation; which preserved the child's life, who after became a Blessing to the Church." The Dr. Tate mentioned above was evidently the Rev. Faithful Tate, D.D., father of Nahum Tate of "Tate and Brady" fame. [9]

On the night of Sunday, the 8th of May 1642, a terrific storm of hail and rain came upon the English soldiers, which of course they attributed to other than the correct source. "All the tents were in a thrice blown over. It was not possible for any match to keep fire, or any sojor to handle his musket or yet to stand. Yea, severalls of them dyed that night of meere cold. Our sojors, and some of our officers too (who suppose that no thing which is more than ordinarie can be the product of nature), attributed this hurrikan to *the divilish skill of some Irish witches.*" [10] Apparently the English were not as wise in their generation as the inhabitants of Constance in Switzerland were on the occasion of a similar ebullition of the elements. The latter went out, found a witch, *persuaded* her to confess herself the guilty author of the storm, and then burnt her—by which time, no doubt, the wind had subsided!

Much in the same strain might be added, but, lest we should weary our readers, we shall content ourselves with giving two more marvellous relations from this particular period so full of the marvellous. O'Daly in his *History of the Geraldines* relates that during the siege of Limerick three portents appeared. The first was a luminous globe, brighter than the moon and little inferior to the sun, which for two leagues and a half shed a vertical light on the city, and then faded into darkness over the enemy's camp; the second was the apparition of the Virgin, accompanied by several of the Saints; and the third was a *lusus naturæ*, of the Siamese-twins type: all three of which O'Daly interprets to his own satisfaction. The first of these was some form of the northern lights, and is also recorded in the diary of certain Puritan officers. That learned, but somewhat too credulous English antiquary, John Aubrey, relates in his *Miscellanies* that before the last battle between the contending parties "a woman of uncommon Statue all in white appearing to the Bishop [Heber McMahon, whom Aubrey terms *Veneras*] admonished him not to cross the River first to assault the Enemy, but suffer them to do it, whereby he should obtain the Victory. That if the *Irish* took the water first to move towards the *English* they should be put to a total Rout, which came to pass. *Ocahan* and. Sir *Henry O'Neal*, who were both killed there, saw severally the same apparition, and dissuaded the Bishop from giving the first onset, but could not prevail upon him."

An instance of an Irishman suffering from the effects of witchcraft outside Ireland is afforded us in a pathetic petition sent up to the English Parliament between the years 1649 and 1653. [11] The petitioner, John Campbell, stated that twelve years since he lost his sight in co. Antrim, where he was born, by which he was reduced to such extremity that he was forced to come over to England to seek some means of livelihood for himself in craving the charity of well-disposed people, but contrary to his expectation he has been often troubled there with dreams and fearful visions in his sleep, and has been twice bewitched, insomuch that he can find no quietness or rest here, and so prays for a pass to return to Ireland.

The saintly James Usher, Archbishop of Armagh, was a Prelate who, if he had happened to live at an earlier period would certainly have been numbered amongst those whose wide and profound learning won for themselves the title of magician—as it was, be was popularly credited with prophetical powers. Most of the prophecies attributed to him may be found in a little pamphlet of eight pages, entitled "Strange and Remarkable Prophecies and Predictions of the Holy, Learned, and Excellent

James Usher, &c... Written by the person who heard it from this Excellent person's own Mouth," and apparently published in 1656. According to it, be foretold the rebellion of 1641 in a sermon on Ezekiel iv. 6, preached in Dublin in

1601. "And of this Sermon the Bishop reserved the Notes, and put a note thereof in the Margent of his Bible, and for twenty years before he still lived in the expectation of the fulfilling thereof, and the nearer the time was the more confident he was that it was nearer accomplishment, though there was no visible appearance of any such thing." He also foretold the death of Charles I, and his own coming poverty and loss of property, which last he actually experienced for many years before his death. The Rev. William Turner in his *Compleat History of Remarkable Providences* (London, 1697 gives a premonition of approaching death that the Archbishop received. A lady who was dead appeare to him in his sleep, and invited him to sup with her the next night. He accepted the invitation, and died the following afternoon, 21st March 1656.

This chapter may be brought to a conclusion by the following story from Glanvill's *Relations*. [12] One Mr. John Browne of Durley in Ireland was made by his neighbour, John Mallett of Enmore, trustee for his children in minority. In 1654 Mr. Browne lay a-dying: at the foot of his bed stood a great iron chest fitted with three locks, in which were the trustees' papers. Some of his people and friends were sitting by him, when to their horror they suddenly saw the locked chest begin to open, lock by lock, without the aid of any visible hand, until at length the lid stood upright. The dying man, who had not spoken for twenty-four hours, sat up in the bed, looked at the chest, and said: *You say true, you say true, you are in the right* (a favourite expression of his), *I'll he with you by and by*, and then lay down again, and never spoke after. The chest slowly locked itself in exactly the same manner as it had opened, and shortly after this Mr. Browne died.

Footnotes

1. Enrolment of Pleas, 6 James I, memb. 2 (Queen's Bench).
2. Scott, *Demonology and Witchcraft*, Letter V.
3. Ed. C. X. Sharpe (Edinburgh, 1818).
4. Witherow, *Memorials of Presbyterianism in Ireland*.
5. Quot. in Law's *Memorialls*.
6. Witherow, *op. cit.*, pp. 15-16.
7. Lenihan, *History of Limerick*, p. 147.
8. Hickson, *Ireland in the Seventeenth Century*, vol. i.; Fitzpatrick, *Bloody Bridge*, p. 125; Temple's *History of the Rebellion*.
9. Baxter, *Certainty of the World of Spirits* (London, 1691); Clark, *A Mirrour or Looking-Glass for Saints and Sinners.* (London, 1657-71).
10. Fitzpatrick, *op. cit.*, p. 127.
11. Hist. MSS. Comm. Report 13 (Duke of Portland MSS.).
12. No. 25 in *Sadducismus Triumphatus* (London, 1726).

CHAPTER V

A.D. 1661

FLORENCE NEWTON, THE WITCH OF YOUGHAL

WITH the Restoration of King Charles II witchcraft did not cease; on the other hand it went on with unimpaired vigour, and several important cases were brought to trial in England. In one instance, at least, it made its appearance in Ireland, this time far south, at Youghal. The extraordinary tale of Florence Newton and her doings, which is related below, forms the seventh Relation in Glanvill's *Sadducismus Triumphatus* (London, 1726); it may also be found, together with some English cases of notoriety, in Francis Bragge's *Witchcraft further displayed* (London, 1712). It is from the first of these sources that we have taken it, and reproduce it here verbatim, except that some redundant matter has been omitted, *i.e.* where one witness relates facts(!) which have already been brought forward as evidence in the examination of a previous witness, and which therefore do not add to our knowledge, though no doubt they materially contributed to strengthen the case against the unfortunate old woman. Hayman in his *Guide to Youghal* attributes the whole affair to the credulity of the Puritan settlers, who were firm believers in such things. In this he is correct no doubt, but it should be borne in mind by the reader that such a belief was not confined to the new-comers at Youghal, but was common property throughout England and Ireland.

The tale shows that there was a little covey of suspected witches in Youghal at that date, as well as some skilful amateur witch-finders (Messrs. Perry, Greatrakes, and Blackwall). From the readiness with which the Mayor proposed to try the "water-experiment" one is led to suspect that such a process as swimming a witch was not altogether unknown in Youghal. For the benefit of the uninitiated we may briefly describe the actual process, which, as we shall see, the Mayor contemplated, but did not actually carry out. The suspected witch is taken, her right thumb tied to her left great toe, and *vice versa*. She is then thrown into the water: if she *sinks* (and drowns, by any chance!) her innocence is conclusively established; if, on the other hand, she *floats*, her witchcraft is proven, for water, as being the element in Baptism, refuses to receive such a sinner in its bosom.

"Florence Newton was committed to Youghal prison by the Mayor of the town, 24th March 1661, for bewitching Mary Longdon, who gave evidence against her at the Cork Assizes (11th September), as follows:

"Mary Longdon being sworn, and bidden to look upon the prisoner, her countenance chang'd pale, and she was very fearful to look towards her, but at last she did, and being asked whether she knew her, she said she did, and wish'd she never had. Being asked how long she had known her, she said for three or four years. And that at Christmas the said Florence came to the Deponent, at the house of John Pyne in Youghal, where the Deponent was a servant, and asked her to give her a piece of Beef out of the Powdering Tub; and the Defendant answering her that she would not give away her Master's Beef, the said Florence seemed to be very angry, and said, *Thou had'st as good give it me*, and went away grumbling.

"That about a week after the Defendant going to the water with a Pail of Cloth on her head she met the said Florence Newton, who came full in her Face, and threw the Pail off her head, and violently kiss'd her, and said, *Mary, I pray thee let thee and I be Friends; for I hear thee no ill will, and I pray thee do thou bear me none*. And that she the Defendant afterwards went home, and that within a few Days after she saw a Woman with a Vail over her Face stand by her bedside, and one standing by her like a little old Man in Silk Cloaths, and that this Man whom she took to be a Spirit drew the Vail off the Woman's Face, and then she knew it to be Goody Newton: and that the Spirit spoke to the Defendant and would have her promise him to follow his advice and she would have all things after her own Heart, to which she says she answered that she would have nothing to say to him, for her trust was in the Lord.

"That within a month after the said Florence had kiss'd her, she this Defendant fell very ill of Fits or Trances, which would take her on a sudden, in that violence that three or four men could not hold her; and in her Fits she would be taken with Vomiting, and would vomit up Needles, Pins, Horsenails, Stubbs, Wooll, and Straw, and that very often. And being asked whether she perceived at these times what she vomited? She replied, she did; for then she was not in so great distraction as in other parts of her Fits she was. And that before the first beginning of her Fits several (and very many) small stones would fall upon her as she went up and down, and would follow her from place to place, and from one Room to another, and would bit her on the head, shoulders, and arms, and fall to the ground and vanish away. And that she and several others would see them both fall upon her and on the ground, but could never take them, save only some few which she and her Master caught in their hands. Amongst which one that had a hole in it she tied (as she was advised) with a leather thong to her Purse, but it was vanish'd immediately, though the latter continu'd tied in a fast knot.

"That in her Fits she often saw Florence Newton, and cried out against her for tormenting of her, for she says, that she would several times Stick Pins into her Arms, and some of them so fast, that a Man must pluck three or four times to get out the Pins, and they were stuck between the skin and the flesh. That sometimes she would be remov'd out of the bed into another Room, sometimes she would be carried to the top of the House, and laid on a board between two Sollar Beams, sometimes put into a Chest, sometimes under a parcel of Wooll, sometimes between two Feather-Beds on which she used to lie, and sometimes between the Bed and the Mat in her Master's Chamber, in the Daytime. And being asked how she knew that she was thus carried about and disposed of, seeing in her Fits she was in a violent distraction? She answered, she never knew where she was, till they of the Family and the Neighbours with them, would be taking her out of the places whither she was so carried and removed. And being asked the reason and wherefore she cried out so much against the said Florence Newton in her Fits? She answered, because she saw her, and felt her torturing her.

"And being asked how she could think it was Florence Newton that did her this prejudice? She said, first, because she threatened her, then because after she had kiss'd her she fell into these Fits, and that she saw and felt her tormenting. And lastly, that when the people of the Family, by advice of the Neighbours and consent of the Mayor, had sent for Florence Newton to come to the Defendant, she was always worse when she was brought to her, and her Fits more violent than at another time. And that after the said Florence was committed at Youghal the Defendant was not troubled, but was very well till a little while after the said Florence was removed to Cork, and then the Defendant was as ill as ever before. And then the Mayor of Youghal, one Mr. Mayre, sent to know whether the said Florence was bolted (as the Defendant was told), and finding she was not, the order was given to put her Bolts on her; which being done, the Deponent saith she was well again, and so hath continued ever since, and being asked whether she had such like Fits before the said Florence gave her the kiss, she saith she never had any, but believed that with the kiss she bewitch'd her, and rather because she had heard from Nicholas Pyne and others that Florence had confessed so much.

"This Mary Longdon having closed her evidence, Florence Newton peeped at her as it were betwixt the heads of the bystanders that interposed between her and the said Mary, and lifting up both her hands together, as they were manacled, cast them in a violent angry motion (as was observed by W. Aston) towards the said Mary, as if she intended to strike at her if she could have reached her, and said, Now she is down. Upon which the Maid fell suddenly down to the ground like a stone, and fell into a most violent Fit, that all the people that could come to lay hands on her could scarce hold her, she biting her own arms and shreeking out in a most hideous manner, to the amazement of all the Beholders. And continuing so for about a quarter of an hour (the said Florence Newton sitting by herself all that while pinching her own hands and arms, as was sworn by some that observed her), the Maid was ordered to be carried out of Court, and taken into a House. Whence several Persons after that brought word, that the Maid was in a Vomiting Fit, and they brought in several crook'd Pins, and Straws, and Wooll, in white Foam like Spittle, in great proportion. Whereupon the Court having taken notice that the Maid said she had been very well when the said Florence was in Bolts, and ill again when out of them, till they were again put on her, demanded of the Jaylor if she were in Bolts or no, to which he said she was not, only manacled. Upon which order was given to put on her Bolts, and upon putting them on she cried out that she was killed, she was undone, she was spoiled, why do you torment me thus? and so continued complaining grievously for half a quarter of an hour. And then came in a messenger from the Maid, and informed the Court the Maid was well. At which Florence immediately and cholerickly uttered these words, *She is not well yet!* And being demanded, how she knew this, she denied she said so, though many in Court heard her say the words, and she said, if she did, she knew not what she said, being old and disquieted, and distracted with her sufferings. But the Maid being reasonably well come to herself, was, before the Court knew anything of it, sent out of Town to Youghall, and so was no further examined.

"The Fit of the Maid being urged by the Court with all the circumstance of it upon Florence Newton, to have been a continuance of her devilish practice, she denied it, and likewise the motion of her hands, and the saying, *Now she is down*, though the Court saw the first, and the words were sworn to by one Roger Moor. And Thomas Harrison swore that be had observed the said Florence peep at her, and use that motion with her hands, and saw the Maid fall immediately upon that motion, and heard the words, Now she is down, uttered.

"Nicholas Stout was next produced by Mr. Attorney-General, who being sworn and examined, saith, That he had often tried her, having heard say that Witches could not say the Lord's Prayer, whether she could or no, and she could not. Whereupon she said she could say it, and had often said it, and the Court being desired by her to hear her say it, gave her leave; and four times together after these words, *Give us this day our daily bread*, she continually said, *As we forgive them*, leaving out altogether the words, *And forgive us our trespasses*, upon which the Court appointed one near her to teach her the words she left out. But she either could not, or would not, say them, using only these or the like words when these were repeated, *Ay, ay, trespasses, that's the word*. And being often pressed to utter the words as they were repeated to her, she did not. And being asked the reason, she said she was old and had a bad memory; and being asked how her memory served her so well for other parts of the Prayer, and only failed her for that, she said she knew not, neither could she help it.

"John Pyne being likewise sworn and examined, saith, That about January last [1661] the said Mary Longdon, being his Servant, was much troubled with small stones that were thrown at her [&c., as in the Deponent's statement, other items of which he also corroborated]. That sometimes the Maid would be reading in a Bible, and on a sudden he hath seen the Bible struck out of her Hand into the middle of the Room, and she immediately cast into a violent Fit. That in the Fits he hath seen two Bibles laid on her Breast, and in the twinkling of an eye they would be cast betwixt the two Beds the Maid lay upon, sometimes thrown into the middle of the Room, and that Nicholas Pyne held the Bible in the Maid's hand so fast, that it being suddenly snatch'd away, two of the leaves were torn.

"Nicholas Pyne being sworn, saith, That the second night after that the Witch had been in Prison, being the 24th [26?] of March last, he and Joseph Thompson, Roger Hawkins, and some others went to, speak with her concerning the Maid, and told her that it was the general opinion of the Town that she had bewitched her, and desired her to deal freely with them, whether she had bewitched her or no. She said she had not *bewitched* her, but it may be she had *overlooked* her, and that there was a great difference between bewitching and overlooking, and that she could not have done her any harm if she had not touch'd her, and that therefore she had kiss'd her. And she said that what mischief she thought of at that time she kiss'd her, that would fall upon her, and that she could not but confess she had wronged the Maid, and thereupon fell down upon her knees, and prayed God to forgive her for wronging the poor Wench. They wish'd that she might not be wholly destroyed by her; to which she said, it must be another that would help her, and not they that did the harm. And then she said, that there were others, as Goody Halfpenny and Goody Dod, in Town, that could do these things as well as she, and that it might be one of these that had done the Maid wrong.

"He further saith, That towards Evening the Door of the Prison shook, and she arose up hastily and said, *What makest thow here this time a night?* And there was a very great noise, as if some body with Bolts and Chains had been running up and down the Room, and they asked her what it was she spoke to, and what it was that made the noise; and she said she saw nothing, neither did she speak, and if she did, it was she knew not what. But the next day she confess'd it was a Spirit, and her Familiar, in the shape of a Greyhound.

"He further saith, That he and Mr. Edward Perry and others for Trial of her took a Tile off the Prison, went to the place where the Witch lay, and carried it to the House where the Maid lived, and put it in the fire until it was red-hot, and then dripped some of the Maid's water upon it, and the Witch was then grievously tormented, and when the water consumed she was well again.

"Edward Perry being likewise sworn, deposeth, That he, Mr. Greatrix, and Mr. Blackwall went to the Maid, and Mr. Greatrix and he had read of a way to discover a Witch, which he would practise. And so they sent for the Witch, and set her on a Stool, and a Shoemaker with a strong Awl endeavoured to stick it into the Stool, but could not till the third time. And then they bade her come off the Stool, but she said she was very weary and could not stir. Then two of them pulled her off, and the Man went to pull out his Awl, and it dropped into his hand with half an Inch broke off the blade of it, and they all looked to have found where it had been stuck, but could find no place where any entry had been made by it. Then they took another Awl, and put it into the Maid's hand, and one of them took the Maid's hand, and ran violently at the Witch's hand with it, but could not enter it, though the Awl was so bent that none of them could put it straight again. Then Mr. Blackwall took a Launce, and launc'd one of her hands an Inch and a half long, and a quarter of an Inch deep, but it bled not at all. Then he launc'd the other hand, and then they bled.

"He further saith, That after she was in Prison he went with Roger Hawkins and others to discourse with the Witch about the Maid, and they asked what it was she spoke to the day before, and after some denial she said it was a Greyhound which was her Familiar, and went out at the Window; and then she said, *If have done the Maid hurt I am sorry for it*. And being asked whether she had done her any hurt she said she never did *bewitch* her, but confess'd she had *overlooked* her, at that time she kiss'd her, but that she could not now help her, for none could help her that did the mishap, but others. Further the Deponent saith, That meeting after the Assizes at Cashel with one William Lap [who suggested the test of the tile, &c.].

"Mr. Wood, a Minister, being likewise sworn and examined, deposeth, That having heard of the stones dropped and thrown at the Maid, and of her Fits, and meeting with the Maid's Brother, he went along with him to the Maid, and found her in her Fit, crying out against Gammer

Newton, that she prick'd and hurt her. And when she came to herself he asked her what had troubled her; and she said Gammer Newton. And the Deponent saith, Why, she was not there. Yes, said she, *I saw her by my bedside*. The Deponent then asked her the original of all, which she related from the time of her begging the Beef, and after kissing, and so to that time. That then they caused the Maid to be got up, and sent for Florence Newton, but she refused to come, pretending she was sick, though it indeed appeared she was well. Then the Mayor of Youghall came in, and spoke with the Maid, and then sent again and caused Florence Newton to be brought in, and immediately the Maid fell into her Fit far more violent, and three times as long as at any other time, and all the time the Witch was in the Chamber the Maid cried out continually of her being hurt here and there, but never named the Witch: but as soon as she was removed, then she cried out against her by the name of Gammer Newton, and this for several times. And still when the Witch was out of the Chamber the Maid would desire to go to Prayers, and he found good affections of her in time of Prayer, but when the Witch was brought in again, though never so privately, although she could not possibly, as the Deponent conceives, see her, she would be immediately senseless, and like to be strangled, and so would continue till the Witch was taken out, and then though never so privately carried away she would come. again to her senses. That afterwards Mr. Greatrix, Mr. Blackwall, and some others, who would need satisfy themselves in the influence of the Witch's presence, tried it and found it several times.

"Richard Mayre, Mayor of Youghall, sworn, saith, That about the 24th of March last he sent for Florence Newton and examined her about the Maid, and she at first denied it, and accused Goodwife Halfpenny and Goodwife Dod, but at length when he had caused a Boat to be provided, and thought to have tried the Water-Experiment on all three, Florence Newton confessed to overlooking. Then he likewise examined the other two Women, but they utterly denied it, and were content to abide any trial; whereupon he caused Dod, Halfpenny, and Newton to be carried to the Maid; and he told her that these two Women, or one of them, were said by Gammer Newton to have done her hurt, but she said, *No, no, they are honest Women, but it is Gammer Newton that hurts me, and I believe she is not far off.* [She was then brought in privately, with the usual result.] He further deposeth that there were three Aldermen in Youghall, whose children she had kiss'd, as he had heard them affirm, and all the children died presently after.

"Joseph Thompson being likewise sworn, saith [the same as Nicholas Pyne relative to the Greyhound-Familiar.]

"Hitherto we have heard the most considerable Evidence touching Florence Newton's witchcraft upon Mary Longdon, for which she was committed to Youghall Prison, 24th March 1661. But April following she bewitched one David Jones to death by kissing his hand through the Grate of the Prison, for which she was indicted at Cork Assizes, and the evidence is as follows:

"Elenor Jones, Relict of the said David Jones, being sworn and examined in open Court what she knew concerning any practice of Witchcraft by the said Florence Newton upon the said David Jones her Husband, gave in Evidence, That in April last the said David, having been out all Night, came home early in the Morning, and said to her, *Where dost thou think I have been all Night?* To which she answered she knew not; whereupon he replied, *I and Frank Beseley have been standing Centinel over the Witch all night.* To which the said Elenor said, *Why, what hurt is that? Hurt?* quoth he. *Marry I doubt it's never a jot the better for me; for she hath kiss'd my Hand, and I have a great pain in that arm, and I verily believe she hath bewitch'd me, if ever she bewitch'd any Man.* To which she answered, *The Lord forbid!* That all that Night, and continually from that time, he was restless and ill, complaining exceedingly of a great pain in his arm for seven days together, and at the seven days' end he complained that the pain was come from his Arm to his Heart, and then kept his bed Night and Day, grievously afflicted, and crying out against Florence Newton, and about fourteen days after he died.

"Francis Beseley being sworn and examined, saith, That about the time aforementioned meeting with the said David Jones, and discoursing with him of the several reports then stirring concerning the said Florence Newton, that she had several Familiars resorting to her in sundry shapes, the said David Jones told him he had a great mind to watch her one Night to see whether he could observe any Cats or other Creatures resort to her through the Grate, as 'twas suspected they did, and desired the said Francis to go with him, which he did. And that when they came thither David Jones came to Florence, and, told her that he heard she could not say the Lord's Prayer; to which she answered, She could. He then desir'd her to say it, but she excused herself by the decay of Memory through old Age. Then David Jones began to teach her, but she could not or would not say it, though often taught it. Upon which the said Jones and Beseley being withdrawn a little from her, and discoursing of her not being able to learn this Prayer, she called out to David Jones, and said, *David, David, come hither, I can say the Lord's Prayer now*. Upon which David went towards her, and the said Deponent would have pluckt him back, and persuaded him not to have gone to her, but he would not be persuaded, but went to the Grate to her, and she began to say the Lord's Prayer, but could not say *Forgive us our trespasses*, so that David again taught her, which she seem'd to take very thankfully, and told him she had a great mind to have kiss'd him, but that the Grate hindered her, but desired she might kiss his Hand; whereupon he gave her his Hand through the Grate, and she kiss'd it; and towards break of Day they went away and parted, and soon after the Deponent heard that David Jones was ill. Whereupon be went to visit him, [and was told by him that the Hag] had him by the Hand, and was pulling off his Arm. And he said, *Do you not see the old hag How she pulls me? Well, I lay my Death on her, she has bewitch'd me.* About fourteen days languishing he died."

This concludes the account of Florence Newton's trial, as given by Glanvill; the source from which it was taken will be alluded to shortly. It would seem that the witch was indicted upon two separate charges, viz. with bewitching the servant-girl, Mary Longdon, and with causing the death of David Jones. The case must have created considerable commotion in Youghal, and was considered so important that the Attorney-General went down to prosecute, but unfortunately there is no record of the verdict. If found guilty (and we can have little doubt but that she was), she would have been sentenced to death in pursuance of the Elizabethan Statute, section i.

Many of the actors in the affair were persons of local prominence, and can be identified. The "Mr. Greatrix" was Valentine Greatrakes, the famous healer or "stroker," who also makes his appearance in the tale of the haunted butler (see p. 164). He was born in 1629, and died in 1683, He joined the Parliamentary Army, and when it was disbanded in 1656, became a country magistrate. At the Restoration he was deprived of his offices, and then gave himself up to a life of contemplation. In 1662 the idea seized him that he had the power of healing the king's-evil. He kept the matter quiet for some time, but at last communicated it to his wife, who jokingly bade him try his power on a boy in the neighbourhood. Accordingly he laid his hands on the affected parts with prayer, and within a month the boy was healed. Gradually his fame spread, until patients came to him from various parts of England as well as Ireland. In 1665 he received an invitation from Lord Conway to come to Ragley to cure his wife of perpetual headaches. He stayed at Ragley about three weeks, and while there he entertained his hosts with the story of Florence Newton and her doings; although he did not succeed in curing Lady Conway, yet many persons in the neighbourhood benefited by his treatment. The form of words he always used was: "God Almighty heal thee for His mercy's sake"; and if the patient professed to receive any benefit he bade them give God the praise. He took no fees, and rejected cases which were manifestly incurable. In modern times the cures have been reasonably attributed to animal magnetism. He was buried beside his father at Affane, co. Waterford. [1] Some of his contemporaries had a very poor opinion of him; Increase Mather, writing in 1684, alludes contemptuously to "the late miracle-monger or Mirabilian stroaker in Ireland, Valentine Greatrix," whom he accuses of attempting to cure an ague by the use of that "hobgoblin word, *Abrodacara*."

John Pyne, the employer of the bewitched servant-girl, served as Bailiff of Youghal along with Edward Perry in 1664, the latter becoming Mayor in 1674; both struck tradesmen's tokens of the usual type. Richard Myres was Bailiff of Youghal in 1642, and Mayor in 1647 and 1660. The Rev. James Wood was appointed "minister of the gospel" at Youghal, by the Commonwealth Government, at a salary Of £120 per annum; in 1654 his stipend was raised to £140, and in the following year he got a further increase of £40. He was sworn in a freeman at large in 1656, and appears to have been presented by the Grand Jury in 1683 as a religious vagrant. [2]

Furthermore, it seems possible to recover the name of the judge who tried the case at the Cork Assizes. Glanvill says that he took the Relation from "a copy of an Authentick Record, as I conceive, every half-sheet having W. Aston writ in the Margin, and then again W. Aston at the end of all, who in all likelihood must be some publick Notary or Record-Keeper." This man, who is also mentioned in the narrative, is to be identified with Judge Sir William Aston, who after the establishment of the Commonwealth came to Ireland, and was there practising as a barrister at the time of the Restoration, having previously served in the royalist army. On 3rd November 1660 he was appointed senior puisne judge of the Chief Place, and died in 1671. [3] The story accordingly is based on the notes taken by the Judge before whom the case was brought, and is therefore of considerable value, in that it affords us a picture, drawn by an eye-witness in full possession of all the facts, of a witch-trial in Ireland in the middle of the seventeenth century.

Footnotes

1. *Dict. Nat. Biog.*
2. *Cork Hist. and Arch. Journal*, vol. x. (2nd series).
3. *Ibid.*, vol. vii. (2nd series).

CHAPTER VI

A.D. 1662-1686

THE DEVIL AT DAMERVILLE—AND AT BALLINAGARDE—TAVERNER AND HADDOCK'S GHOST—HUNTER AND THE GHOSTLY OLD WOMAN—A WITCH RESCUED BY THE DEVIL—DR. WILLIAMS AND THE HAUNTED HOUSE IN DUBLIN—APPARITIONS SEEN IN THE AIR IN CO. TIPPERARY—A CLERGYMAN AND HIS WIFE BEWITCHED TO DEATH—BEWITCHING OF MR. MOOR—THE FAIRY-POSSESSED BUTLER—A GHOST INSTIGATES A PROSECUTION—SUPPOSED WITCHCRAFT IN CO. CORK—THE DEVIL AMONG THE QUAKERS.

FROM the earliest times the Devil has made his mark, historically and geographically, in Ireland; the nomenclature of many places indicates that they are his exclusive property, while the antiquarian cannot be sufficiently thankful to him for depositing the Rock of Cashel where he did. But here we must deal with a later period of his activity. A quaint tale comes to us from co. Tipperary of a man bargaining with his Majesty for the price of his soul, in which as usual the Devil is worsted by a simple trick, and gets nothing for his trouble. Near Shronell in that county are still to be seen the ruins of Damerville Court, formerly the residence of the Damer family, and from which locality they took the title of Barons Milton of Shronell. The first of the family to settle in Ireland, Joseph Damer, had been formerly in the service of the Parliament, but not deeming it safe to remain in England after the Restoration, came over to this country and, taking advantage of the cheapness of land at that time, Purchased large estates. It was evidently of this member of the family that the following tale is told. He possessed great wealth, and 'twas darkly hinted that this had come to him from no lawful source, that in fact he had made a bargain with the Devil to sell his soul to him for a top-boot full of gold. His Satanic Majesty greedily accepted the offer, and on the day appointed for the ratification of the bargain arrived with a sufficiency of bullion from the Bank of Styx—or whatever may be the name of the establishment below! He was ushered into a room, in the middle of which stood the empty top-boot; into this he poured the gold, but to his surprise it remained as empty as before. He hastened away for more gold, with the same result. Repeated journeys to and fro for fresh supplies still left the boot as empty as when he began, until at length in sheer disgust he took his final departure, leaving Damer in possession of the gold, and as well (for a few brief years, at all events) of that spiritual commodity he had valued at so little. In process of time the secret leaked out. The wily Damer had taken the sole off the boot, and had then securely fastened the latter over a hole in the floor. In the storey underneath was a series of large, empty cellars, in which he had stationed men armed with shovels, who were under instructions to remove each succeeding shower of gold, and so make room for more.

Another story [1] comes from Ballinagarde in co. Limerick. the residence of the Croker family, though it is probably later in point of time; in it the Devil appears in a different rôle. Once upon a time Mr. Croker of Ballinagarde was out hunting, but as the country was very difficult few were able to keep up with the hounds. The chase lasted all day, and late in the evening Croker and a handsome dark stranger, mounted on a magnificent black horse, were alone at the death. Croker, delighted at his companion's prowess, asked him home, and the usual festivities were kept up fast and furious till far into the night. The stranger was shown to a bedroom, and as the servant was pulling off his boots he saw that he had a cloven hoof. In the morning he acquainted his master with the fact, and both went to see the stranger. The latter had disappeared, and so had his horse, but the bedroom carpet was seared by a red-hot hoof, while four hoof-marks were imprinted on the floor of the horse's stall. What incident gave rise to the story we cannot tell, but there was a saying among the peasantry that such-and-such a thing occurred "as sure as the Devil was in Ballinagarde"; while he is said to have appeared there again recently.

A most remarkable instance of legal proceedings being instituted at the instigation of a ghost comes from the co. Down in the year 1662. [2] About Michaelmas one Francis Taverner, servant to Lord Chichester, was riding home on horseback late one night from Hillborough, and on nearing Drumbridge his horse suddenly stood still, and he, not suspecting anything out of the common, but merely supposing him to have the staggers, got down to bleed him in the mouth, and then remounted. As he was proceeding two horsemen seemed to pass him, though he heard no sound of horses' hoofs. Presently there appeared a third at his elbow, apparently clad in a long white coat, having the appearance of one James Haddock, an inhabitant of Malone who had died about five years previously. When the startled Taverner asked him in God's name who he was, he told him that he was James Haddock, and recalled himself to his mind by relating a trifling incident that had occurred in Taverner's father's house a short while before Haddock's death. Taverner asked him why he spoke with him he told him, because he was a man of more resolution than other men, and requested him to ride along with him in order that he might acquaint him with the business he desired him to perform. Taverner refused, and, as they were at a cross-road, went his own way. Immediately after parting with the spectre there arose a mighty wind, "and withal he heard very hideous Screeches and Noises, to his great amazement. At last he heard the cocks crow, to his great comfort; he alighted off his horse, and falling to prayer desired God's assistance, and so got safe home."

The following night the ghost appeared again to him as he sat by the fire, and thereupon declared to him the reason for its appearance, and the errand upon which it wished to send him. It bade him go to Eleanor Walsh, its widow, who was now married to one Davis, and say to her that it was the will of her late husband that their son David should be righted in the matter of a lease which the father had bequeathed to him, but of which the step-father had unjustly deprived him. Taverner refused to do so, partly because he did not desire to gain the ill-will of his neighbours, and partly because he feared being taken for one demented; but the ghost so thoroughly frightened him by appearing to him every night for a month, that in the end he promised to fulfil its wishes. He went to Malone, found a woman named Eleanor Walsh, who proved to be the wrong person, but who told him she had a namesake living hard by, upon which Taverner took no further trouble in the matter, and returned without delivering his message.

The same night he was awakened by something pressing upon him, and saw again the ghost of Haddock in a white coat, which asked him if he had delivered the message, to which Taverner mendaciously replied that he had been to Malone and had seen Eleanor Walsh. Upon which the ghost looked with a more friendly air upon him, bidding him not to be afraid, and then vanished in a flash of brightness. But having learnt the truth of the matter in some mysterious way, it again appeared, this time in a great fur and threatened to tear him to pieces if he did not do as it desired. Utterly unnerved by these unearthly visits, Taverner left his house in the mountains and went into the town of Belfast, where he sat up all night in the house of a shoemaker named Peirce, where were also two or three of Lord Chichester's servants. "About midnight, as they were all by the fireside, they beheld Taverner's countenance change and a trembling to fall upon him; who presently espied the Apparition in a Room opposite him, and took up the Candle and went to it, and resolutely ask'd it in the name of God wherefore it haunted him? It replied, Because he had not delivered the message; and withal repeated the threat of tearing him in pieces if he did not do so speedily: and so, changing itself into many prodigious Shapes, it vanished in white like a Ghost."

In a very dejected frame of mind Taverner related the incident to some of Lord Chichester's family, and the chaplain, Mr. James South, advised him to go and deliver the message to the widow, which he accordingly did, and thereupon experienced great quietness of mind. Two nights later the apparition again appeared, and on learning what had been done, charged him to bear the same message to the executors. Taverner not unnaturally asked if Davis, the step-father, would attempt to do him any harm, to which the spirit gave a very doubtful response, but at length reassured him by threatening Davis if he should attempt anything to his injury, and then vanished away in white.

The following day Taverner was summoned before the Court of the celebrated Jeremy Taylor, Bishop of Down, who carefully examined him about the matter, and advised him the next time the spirit appeared to ask it the following questions: Whence are you? Are you a good or a bad spirit? Where is your abode? What station do you hold? How are you regimented in the other world? What is the reason that you appear for the relief of your son in so small a matter, when so many widows and orphans are oppressed, and none from thence of their relations appear as you do to right them?

That night Taverner went to Lord Conway's house. Feeling the coming presence of the apparition, and being unwilling to create any disturbance within doors, he and his brother went out into the courtyard, where they saw the spirit coming over the wall. He told it what he had done, and it promised not to trouble him any more, but threatened the executors if they did not see the boy righted. "Here his brother put him in mind to ask the Spirit what the Bishop bid him, which he did presently. But it gave him no answer, but crawled on its hands and feet over the wall again, and so vanished in white with a most melodious harmony." The boy's friends then brought an action (apparently in the Bishop's Court) against the executors and trustees; one of the latter, John Costlet, who was also the boy's uncle, tried the effect of bluff, but the threat of what the apparition could and might do to him scared him into a promise of justice. About five years later, when the story was forgotten, Costlet began to threaten the boy with an action, but, coming home drunk one night, he fell off his horse and was killed. In the above there is no mention of the fate of Davis.

Whatever explanation we may choose to give of the *supernatural* element in the above, there seems to be no doubt that such an incident occurred, and that the story is, in the main, true to fact, as it was taken by Glanvill from a letter of Mr. Thomas Alcock's, the secretary to Bishop Taylor's Court, who must therefore have heard the entire story from Taverner's own lips. The incident is vividly remembered in local tradition, from which many picturesque details are added, especially with reference to the trial, the subsequent righting of young David Haddock, and the ultimate punishment of Davis, on which points Glanvill is rather unsatisfactory. According to this source, [3] Taverner (or Tavney, as the name is locally pronounced) *felt something get up behind him* as he was riding home, and from the eerie feeling that came over him, as well as from the mouldy smell of the grave that assailed his nostrils, he perceived that his companion was not of this world. Finally the ghost urged Taverner to bring the case into Court, and it came up for trial at Carrickfergus. The Counsel for the opposite side browbeat Taverner for inventing such an absurd and malicious story about his neighbour Davis, and ended by tauntingly desiring him to call his witness. The usher of the Court, with a sceptical sneer, called upon James Haddock, and at the third repetition of the name a clap of thunder shook the Court; a hand was seen on the witness-table, and a voice was heard saying, "Is this enough?" Which very properly convinced the jury. Davis slunk away, and on his homeward road fell from his horse and broke his neck. Instead of propounding Bishop Taylor's shorter catechism, Taverner merely asked the ghost, "Are you happy in your present state?" "If," it replied in a voice of anger, "you were not the man you are, I would tear you in pieces for asking such a question"; and then went off in a flash of fire!!—which, we fear, afforded but too satisfactory an answer to his question.

In the following year, 1663, a quaintly humorous story [4] of a most persistent and troublesome ghostly visitant comes from the same part of the world, though in this particular instance its efforts to right the wrong did not produce a lawsuit: the narrator was Mr. Alcock, who appears in the preceding story. One David Hunter, who was neat-herd to the Bishop of Down (Jeremy Taylor) at his house near Portmore, saw one night, as he was carrying a log of wood into the dairy, an old woman whom he did not recognise, but apparently some subtle intuition told him that she was not of mortal mould, for incontinent he flung away the log, and ran terrified into his house. She appeared again to him the next night, and from that on nearly every night for the next nine months. "Whenever she came he must go with her through the Woods at a good round rate; and the poor fellow look'd as if he was bewitch'd and travell'd off his legs." Even if be were in bed he had to rise and follow her wherever she went, and because his wife could not restrain him she would rise and follow him till daybreak, although no apparition was visible to her. The only member of the family that took the matter philosophically was Hunter's little dog, and he became so accustomed to the ghost that he would inevitably bring up the rear of the strange procession—if it be true that the lower classes dispensed with the use of night-garments when in bed, the sight must truly have been a most remarkable one.

All this time the ghost afforded no indication as to the nature and object of her frequent appearances. "But one day the said David going over a Hedge into the Highway, she came just against him, and he cry'd out, 'Lord bless me, I would I were dead; shall I never be delivered from this misery?' At which, 'And the Lord bless me too,' says she. 'It was very happy you spoke first, for till then I had no power to speak, though I have followed you so long. My name,' says she, 'is Margaret—. I lived here before the War, and had one son by my Husband; when he died

I married a soldier, by whom I had several children which the former Son maintained, else we must all have starved. He lives beyond the Banwater; pray go to him and bid him dig under such a hearth, and there he shall find 28s. Let him pay what I owe in such a place, and the rest to the charge unpay'd at my Funeral, and go to my Son that lives here, which I had by my latter Husband, and tell him that he lives a very wicked and dissolute life, and is very unnatural and ungrateful to his Brother that nurtured him, and if he does not mend his life God will destroy him.'"

David Hunter told her he never knew her. "No," says she, "I died seven years before you came into this Country"; but she promised that, if he would carry her message, she would never hurt him. But he deferred doing what the apparition bade him, with the result that she appeared the night after, as he lay in bed, and struck him on the shoulder very hard; at which he cried out, and reminded her that she had promised to do him no hurt. She replied that was if he did her message; if not, she would kill him. He told her he could not go now, because the waters were out. She said that she was content that he should wait until they were abated; but charged him afterwards not to fail her. Ultimately be did her errand, and afterwards she appeared and thanked him. "For now," said she, "I shall be at rest, and therefore I pray you lift me up from the ground, and I will trouble you no more." So Hunter lifted her up, and declared afterwards that she felt just like a bag of feathers in his arms; so she vanished, and he heard most delicate music as she went off over his head.

An important witch-case occurred in Scotland in 1678, the account of which is of interest to us as it incidentally makes mention of the fact that one of the guilty persons had been previously tried and condemned in Ireland for the crime of witchcraft. Four women and one man were strangled and burnt at Paisley for having attempted to kill by magic Sir George Maxwell of Pollock. They had formed a wax image of him, into which the Devil himself had stuck the necessary pins; it was then turned on a spit before the fire, the entire band repeating in unison the name of him whose death they desired to compass. Amongst the women was "one Bessie Weir, who was hanged up the last of the four (*one that had been taken before in Ireland and was condemned to the fyre for malifice before*; and when the hangman there was about to cast her over the gallows, the devill takes her away from them out of their sight; her *dittay* [indictment] was sent over here to Scotland), who at this tyme, when she was cast off the gallows, there appears a raven, and approaches the hangman within an ell of him, and flyes away again. All the people observed it, and cried out at the sight of it." [5]

A clergyman, the Rev. Daniel Williams (evidently the man who was pastor of Wood Street, Dublin, and subsequently founded Dr. Williams's Library in London), relates the manner in which he freed a girl from strange and unpleasant noises which disturbed her; the incident might have developed into something analogous to the Drummer of Tedworth in England, but on the whole works out rather tamely. He tells us that about the year 1678 the niece of Alderman Arundel of Dublin was troubled by noises in her uncle's house, "as by violent Sthroaks on the Wainscots and Chests, in what Chambers she frequented." In the hope that they would cease she removed to a house near Smithfield, but the disturbances pursued her thither, and were no longer heard in her former dwelling. She thereupon betook herself to a little house in Patrick Street, near the gate, but to no purpose. The noises lasted in all for about three months, and were generally at their worst about two o'clock in the morning. Certain ministers spent several nights in prayer with her, heard the strange sounds, but did not succeed in causing their cessation. Finally the narrator, Williams, was called in, and came upon a night agreed to the house, where several persons had assembled. He says: "I preached from Hebrews ii. 18, and contrived to be at Prayer at that Time when the Noise used to be greatest. When I was at Prayer the Woman, kneeling by me, catched violently at my Arm, and afterwards told us that she raw a terrible Sight—but it pleased God there was no noise at all. And from that Time God graciously freed her from all that Disturbance." [6]

Many strange stories of apparitions seen in the air come from all parts of the world, and are recorded by writers both ancient and modern, but there are certainly few of them that can equal the account of that weird series of incidents that was seen in the sky by a goodly crowd of ladies and gentlemen in co. Tipperary on 2nd March 1678. [7] "At Poinstown in the county of Tepperary were seen divers strange and prodigious apparitions. On Sunday in the evening several gentlemen and others, after named, walked forth in the fields, and the Sun going down, and appearing somewhat bigger than usual, they discoursed about it, directing their eyes towards the place where the Sun set; when one of the company observed in the air, near the place where the Sun went down, an Arm of a blackish blue colour, with a ruddy complection'd Hand at one end, and at the other end a cross piece with a ring fasten'd to the middle of it, like one end of an anchor, which stood still for a while, and then made northwards, and so disappeared. Next, there appeared at a great distance in the air, from the same part of the sky, something like a Ship coming towards them; and it came so near that they could distinctly perceive the masts, sails, tacklings, and men; she then seem'd to tack about, and sail'd with the stern foremost, northwards, upon a dark smooth sea, which stretched itself from south-west to north-west. Having seem'd thus to sail some few minutes she sunk by degrees into the sea, her stern first; and as she sunk they perceived her men plainly running up the tacklings in the forepart of the Ship, as it were to save themselves from drowning. Then appeared a Fort, with somewhat like a Castle on the top of it; out of the sides of which, by reason of some clouds of smoak and a flash of fire suddenly issuing out, they concluded some shot to be made. The Fort then was immediately divided in two parts, which were in an instant transformed into two exact Ships, like the other they had seen, with their heads towards each other. That towards the south seem'd to chase the other with its stem [stern?] foremost, northwards, till it sunk with its stem first, as the, first Ship had done; the other Ship sail'd some time after, and then sunk with its head first. It was observ'd that men were running upon the decks of these two Ships, but they did not see them climb up, as in the last Ship, excepting one man, whom they saw distinctly to get up with much haste upon the very top of the Bowsprit of the second Ship as they were sinking. They supposed the two last Ships were engaged, and fighting, for they saw the likeness of bullets rouling upon the sea, while they were both visible. Then there appear'd a Chariot, drawn with two horses, which turn'd as the Ships had done, northward, and immediately after it came a strange frightful creature, which they concluded to be some kind of serpent, having a head like a snake, and a knotted bunch or bulk at the other end, something resembling a snail's house. This monster came swiftly behind the chariot and gave it a sudden violent blow, then out of the chariot leaped a Bull and a Dog, which follow'd him [the bull], and seem'd to bait him. These also went northwards, as the former had done, the Bull first, holding his head downwards, then the Dog, and then the Chariot, till all sunk down one after another about the same place, and just in the same manner as the former. These meteors being vanished, there were several appearances like ships and other things. The whole time of the vision lasted near an hour, and it was a very clear and calm evening, no cloud seen, no mist, nor any wind stirring. All the phenomena came out of the West or Southwest, and all moved Northwards; they all sunk out of sight much about the same place. Of the whole company there was not any one but saw all these things, as above-written, whose names follow:

> "'Mr. Allye, a minister, living near the place.
> Lieutenant Dunsterville, and his son. Mr. Grace, his son-in-law.
> Lieutenant Dwine. Mr. Dwine, his brother.
> Mr.. Christopher Hewelson. Mr. Richard Foster.
> Mr. Adam Hewelson.
> Mr. Bates, a schoolmaster.
> Mr. Larkin.
> Mrs. Dunsterville.
> Her daughter-in-law.
> Her maiden daughter.
> Mr. Dwine's daughter.
> Mrs. Grace, her daughter."

The first of the sixteen persons who subscribed to the truth of the above was the Rev. Peter Alley, who had been appointed curate of Killenaule Union (Dio. Cashel) in 1672, but was promoted to livings in the same diocese in the autumn of the year the apparitions appeared. [8] There is a townland named Poyntstown in the parish of Buolick and barony of Slievardagh, and another of the same name in the adjoining parish of Fennor. It must have been at one or other of these places that the sights were witnessed, as both parishes are only a few miles distant from Killenaule. Somewhat similar tales, although not so full of marvellous detail, are reported at different periods from the west of Ireland. Such indeed seem to have been the origin of the belief in that mysterious island O'Brasil, lying far out in the western ocean. About the year 1665, a Quaker pretended that he had a revelation from Heaven that he was the man ordained to discover it, and accordingly fitted out a ship for the purpose. In 1674, Captain John Nisbet, formerly of co. Fermanagh, actually landed there! At this period it was located off Ulster. [9]

Between the clergy and the witches a continuous state of warfare existed; the former, both Protestant and Roman Catholic, ever assumed the offensive, and were most diligent in their attempts to eradicate such a damnable heresy from the world—indeed with regret it must be confessed that their activity in this respect was frequently the means of stirring up the quiescent Secular Arm, thereby setting on foot bloody persecutions, in the course of which many innocent creatures were tortured and put to a cruel death. Consequently, human nature being what it is, it is not a matter of surprise to learn that witches occasionally appear as the aggressors, and cause the clergy as much uneasiness of mind and body as they possibly could. In or about the year 1670 an Irish clergyman, the Rev. James Shaw, Presbyterian minister of Carnmoney, "was much troubled with witches, one of them appearing in his chamber and showing her face behind his cloke hanging on the clock-pin, and then stepping to the door, disappeared. He was troubled with cats coming into his chamber and bed; be sickens and dyes; his wyfe being dead before him, and, as was supposed, witched." Some equally unpleasant experiences befel his servant. "Before his death his man going out to the stable one night, sees as if it had been a great heap of hay rolling towards him, and then appeared in the shape and likeness of a bair [bear]. He charges it to appear in human shape, which it did. Then he asked, for what cause it troubled him? It bid him come to such a place and it should tell him, which he ingaged to do, yet ere be did it, acquainted his master with it; his master forbids him to keep sic a tryst; he obeyed his master, and went not. That night he should have kept, there is a stone cast at him from the roof of the house, and only touches him, but does not hurt him; whereupon he conceives that had been done to him by the devill, because he kept not tryst; wherefore he resolutely goes forth that night to the place appointed, being a rash bold fellow, and the divill appears in human shape, with his heid running down with blood. He asks him again, why he troubles him? The devill replyes, that he was the spirit of a murdered man who lay under his bed, and buried in the ground, and who was murdered by such a man living in sic a place twenty years ago. The man comes home, searches the place, but finds nothing of bones or anything lyke a grave, and causes send to such a place to search for such a man, but no such a one could be found, and shortly after this man dyes." To which story Mr. Robert Law [10] sagely adds the warning: "It's not good to come in communing terms with Satan, there is a snare in the end of it, but to resyst him by prayer and faith and to turn a deaf ear to his temptations."

Whatever explanation we may choose to give of the matter, there is no doubt but at the time the influence of witchcraft was firmly believed in, and the deaths of Mr. Shaw and his wife attributed to supernatural and diabolical sources. The Rev. Patrick Adair, a distinguished contemporary and co-religionist of Mr. Shaw, alludes to the incident as follows in his *True Narrative*: "There had been great ground of jealousy that she [Mrs. Shaw] in her child-bed had been wronged by sorcery of some witches in the parish. After her death, a considerable time, some spirit or spirits troubled the house by casting stones down at the chimney, appearing to the servants, and especially having got one of them, a young man, to keep appointed times and places, wherein it appeared in divers shapes, and spake audibly to him. The people of the parish watched the house while Mr. Shaw at this time lay sick in his bed, and indeed he did not wholly recover, but within a while died, it was thought not without the art of sorcery."

Classon Porter in his pamphlet gives an interesting account of the affair, especially of the trend of events between the deaths of the husband and wife respectively; according to this source the servant-boy was an accomplice of the Evil One, not a foolish victim. Mrs. Shaw was dead, and Mr. Shaw lay ill, and so was unable to go to the next monthly meeting of his brethren in the ministry to consult them about these strange occurrences. However, he sent his servant, who was supposed to be implicated in these transactions, with a request that his brethren would examine him about the matter, and deal with him as they thought best. The boy was accordingly questioned on the subject, and having confessed that he had conversed and conferred with the evil spirit, and even assisted it in its diabolical operations, he was commanded for the future to have no dealings of any kind with that spirit. The boy promised obedience, and was dismissed. But the affair made a great commotion in the parish, so great that the brethren not only ordered the Communion (which was then approaching) to be delayed in Carnmoney "until the confusion should fall a little," but appointed two of their number to hold a special fast in the congregation of Carnmoney, "in consideration of the trouble which had come upon the minister's house by a spirit that appeared to some of the family, and the distemper of the minister's own body, with other confusions that had followed this movement in the parish." The ministers appointed to this duty were, Kennedy of Templepatrick, and Patton of Ballyclare, who reported to the next meeting that they had kept the fast at Carnmoney, but with what result is not stated. Mr. Shaw died about two months later.

Most wonderful and unpleasant were the bodily contortions that an Irish gentleman suffered, as the result of not having employed a woman who to the useful trade of *sage-femme* added the mischievous one of witch—it is quite conceivable that a country midwife, with some little knowledge of medicine and the use of simples, would be classed in popular opinion amongst those who had power above the average. "In Ireland there was one Thomas Moor, who had his wife brought to bed of a child, and not having made use of her former midwife, who was *malæ famæ*, she was witched by her so that she dies. The poor man resenting it, she was heard to say that that was nothing to that which should follow. She witches him also, so that a certain tyme of the day, towards night, the Devil did always trouble him, once every day for the space of 10 or 12 yeirs, by possessing his body, and causing it to swell highly, and tearing him so that he foamed, and his face turned about to his neck, having a most fearfull disfigured visage. At which tyme he was held by strong men, out of whose grips when he gott, he would have rushed his head against the wall in hazard of braining himself, and would have leaped up and down fearfully, tumbling now and then on the ground, and cryed out fearfully with a wyld skirle and noise, and this he did ordinarily for the space of ane hour; when the fitt was over he was settled as before; and without the fitt he was in his right mynd, and did know when it came on him, and gave notice of it, so that those appoynted for keeping of him prepared for it. He was, by appointment of the ministers, sent from parish to parish for the case of his keepers. At length, people being wearied with waiting on him, they devysed a way for ease, which was to put him in a great chyer [chair] fitted for receiving of his body, and so ordered it that it clasped round about so that he could not get out, and then by a pillue [pulley] drew him up off the ground; and when the fitt came on (of whilk he still gave warning) put him in it and drew him up, so that his swinging to and froo did not hurt him, but was keept till the fitt went over save fra danger, and then lett down till that tyme of the next day, when the fitt recurred. Many came to see him in his fitts, but the sight was so astonishing that few desired to come again. He was a man of a good report, yet we may see givin up to Satan's molestations by the wise and soveraigne God. Complains were givin in against her [the midwife] for her malefices to the magistrat there, but in England and Ireland they used not to judge and condemn witches upon presumptions, but are very sparing as to that. He was alive in the year 1679." The concluding words of the story would lead us to infer that trials for witchcraft had taken place in Ireland, of which Law had heard, and from the report of which he formed his opinion relative to the certain amount of commonsense displayed by the magistrates in that country, in contradistinction to Scotland, where the very slightest evidence sufficed to bring persons to torture and death.

In the following tale [11] the ghostly portion is rather dwarfed by the strong fairy element which appears in it, and, as we have already shown, many witchcraft cases in Scotland were closely interwoven with the older belief in the "good people"; Lord Orrery, when giving the account to Baxter, considered it to be "the effect of Witchcraft or Devils." The reader is free to take what view he likes of the matter! The Lord Orrery mentioned therein is probably Roger, the second Earl, whom Lodge in his *Peerage* describes as being "of a serious and contemplative disposition, which led him to seek retirement." If this identification be correct the following event must have occurred between 1679 and 1682, during which years the Earl held the title.

The butler of a gentleman living near the Earl was sent to buy a pack of cards, As he was crossing a field he was surprised to see a company of people sitting down at a table loaded with all manner of good things, of which they invited him to partake, and no doubt he would have accepted had not someone whispered in his ear, "Do nothing this company invites you to," upon which he refused. After this they first fell to dancing, and playing on musical instruments, then to work, in both of which occupations they desired the butler to join, but to no purpose.

The night following the friendly spirit came to his bedside and warned him not to stir out of doors the next day, for if he did so the mysterious company would obtain possession of him. He remained indoors the greater part of that day, but towards evening he crossed the threshold, and hardly had he done so when a rope was cast about his waist, and he was forcibly dragged away with great swiftness. A horseman coming towards him espied both the man and the two ends of the rope, but could see nothing pulling. By catching hold of one end he succeeded in stopping the man's headlong course, though as a punishment for so doing he received a smart blow on his arm from the other.

This came to the ears of the Earl of Orrery, who requested the butler's master to send him to his house, which the latter did. There were then staying with the Earl several persons of quality, two Bishops, and the celebrated Healer, Valentine Greatrakes. Here the malice of the spirits or fairies manifested itself in a different manner. The unfortunate man was suddenly perceived to rise from the ground, and the united efforts of Greatrakes and another were unable to check his upward motion—in fact all that the spectators could do was to keep running under him to protect him from being hurt if the invisible power should suddenly relax its hold. At length he fell, but was caught by them before he reached the ground, and so received no harm.

That night the spectre, which had twice proved so friendly, appeared at his bedside with a wooden platter full of some grey liquid, which it bade him drink, as he had brought it to him to cure him of two sorts of fits he was subject to. He refused to drink it, and it would appear from another part of the narration that his refusal was based on the advice of the two Bishops, whom he had consulted in the matter. At this the spirit was very angry, but told him he had a kindness for him, and that if he drank the juice of plantain-roots he would be cured of one sort of fit, but that he should suffer the other one till his death. On asking his visitant who he was, he replied that he was the ghost of a man who had been dead seven years, and who in the days of his flesh had led a loose life, and was therefore condemned to be borne about in a restless condition with the strange company until the Day of judgment. He added that "if the butler had acknowledged God in all His ways he had not suffered such things by their means," and reminded him that he had not said his prayers the day before he met the company in the field; and thereupon vanished. Had this story rested alone on the evidence of the butler the "two sorts of fits" would have been more than sufficient to account for it, but what are we to say to the fact that all the main points of the narrative were borne out by the Earl, while Mr. Greatrakes (according to Dr. More, the author of *Collections of Philosophical Writings*) declared that he was actually an eye-witness of the man's being carried in the air above their heads.

At the instigation of a ghost a lawsuit took place at Downpatrick in 1685. The account of this was given to Baxter [12] by Thomas Emlin, "a worthy preacher in Dublin," as well as by Claudius Gilbert, one of the principal parties therein concerned: the latter's son and namesake proved a liberal benefactor to the Library of Trinity College—some of his books have been consulted for the present work. It appears that for some time past there had been a dispute about the tithes of Drumbeg, a little parish about four miles outside Belfast, between Mr. Gilbert, who was vicar of that town, and the Archdeacon of Down, Lemuel Matthews, whom Cotton in his *Fasti* describes as "a man of considerable talents and legal knowledge, but of a violent overbearing temper, and a litigous disposition." The parishioners of Drumbeg favoured Gilbert, and generally paid the tithes to him as being the incumbent in possession; but the Archdeacon claimed to be the lawful recipient, in support of which claim he produced a warrant. In the execution of this by his servants at the house of Charles Lostin, one of the parishioners, they offered some violence to his wife Margaret, who refused them entrance, and who died about a month later (1st Nov. 1685) of the injuries she had received at their hands. Being a woman in a bad state of health little notice was taken of her death, until about a month after she appeared to one Thomas Donelson, who had been a spectator of the violence done her, and "affrighted him into a Prosecution of Robert Eccleson, the Criminal. She appeared divers times, but chiefly upon one Lord's Day-Evening, when she fetch'd him with a strange force out of his House into the Yard and Fields adjacent. Before her last coming (for she did so three times that Day) several Neighbours were called in, to whom he gave notice that she was again coming; and beckon'd him to come out; upon which they went to shut the Door, but he forbad it, saying that she looked with a terrible Aspect upon him, when they offered it. But his Friends laid hold on him and embraced him, that he might not go out again; notwithstanding which (a plain evidence of some invisible Power), he was drawn out of their Hands in a surprizing manner, and carried about into the Field and Yard, as before, she charging him to prosecute Justice: which Voice, as also Donelson's reply, the people heard, though they saw no shape. There are many Witnesses of this yet alive, particularly Sarah (Losnam), the Wife of Charles Lostin, Son to the deceased Woman, and one William Holyday and his Wife." This last appearance took place in Holyday's house; there were also present several young persons, as well as Charles and Helen Lostin, children of the deceased, most of whom appeared as witnesses at the trial.

Upon this Donelson deposed all he knew of the matter to Mr. Randal Brice, a neighbouring justice of the Peace; the latter brought the affair before the notice of Sir William Franklin in Belfast Castle. The depositions were subsequently carried to Dublin, and the case was tried at Downpatrick Assizes by judge John Lindon in 1685. [13] On behalf of the plaintiff, Charles Lostin, Counseller James Macartney acted—if he be the judge who subsequently makes his appearance in a most important witch-trial at Carrickfergus, he certainly was as excellent an advocate as any plaintiff in a case of witchcraft could possibly desire, as he was strongly prejudiced in favour of the truth of all such matters. "The several Witnesses were heard and sworn, and their Examinations were entred in the Record of that Assizes, to the Amazement and Satisfaction of all that Country and of the judges, whom I have heard speak of it at that time with much Wonder; insomuch that the said Eccleson hardly escaped with his life, but was Burnt in the Hand."

A case of supposed witchcraft occurred in Cork in 1685-6, the account of which is contained in a letter from Christopher Crofts to Sir John Perceval (the third Baronet, and father of the first Earl of Egmont) written on the fifteenth of March in that year. Though the narrator professes his disbelief in such superstitions, yet there seems to have been an unconscious feeling in his mind that his strict administration of the law was the means of bringing the affliction on his child. He says: "My poor boy Jack to all appearances lay dying; he had a convulsion for eight or nine hours. His mother and several others are of opinion he is bewitched, and by the old woman, the mother of Nell Welsh, who is reputed a bad woman; and the child was playing by her that day she was upon her examination, and was taken ill presently after she was committed to Bridewell. But I have not faith to believe it was anything but the hand of God. I have committed the girl to Bridewell, where she shall stay some time." 14

At one period in their history that peculiar people, known amongst themselves as the Society of Friends, and by their opponents as Quakers, appear to have been most troublesome, and to have caused a good deal of annoyance to other religious bodies. Not unnaturally their enemies credited any wild tales which were related about them to their detriment, especially when they had reference to their doctrine of the influence of the Spirit. Dr. More, in his continuation to Glanvill's book, has in the sixth Relation an account of a man, near Cambridge in England, who was possessed by an evil spirit which led him to do the most extraordinary things in its attempt to convert him to Quakerism. In the *Life of Mr. Alexander Peden, late Minister of the Gospel at New Glenluce in Galloway*, who died in 1686, there is an account of a Quakers' meeting in this country at which the Devil appeared in most blasphemous parody of the Holy Ghost. As Mr. Peden was travelling one time by himself in Ireland "the night came on, and a dark mist, which obliged him to go into a house belonging to a Quaker. Mr. Peden said, 'I must beg the favour of the roof of your house all night.' The Quaker said, 'Thou art a stranger, thou art very welcome and shalt be kindly entertained, but I cannot wait upon thee, for I am going to the meeting.' Mr. Peden said, 'I will go along with you. The Quaker said, 'Thou may, if thou please, but thou must not trouble us.' He said, 'I will be civil.' When they came to the meeting, as their ordinary is, they sat for some time silent, some with their faces to the wall, and others covered. There being a void in the loft above them there came down the appearance of a raven, and sat upon one man's head, who started up immediately, and spoke with such vehemence that the froth flew from his mouth; it went to a second, and he did the same; and to a third, who did as the former two. Mr. Peden sitting near to his landlord said, 'Do you not see that? Ye will not deny it afterwards?' When they dismissed, going home Mr. Peden said to him, 'I always thought there was devilry among you, but never thought that he did appear visibly among you till now that I have seen it.' The poor man fell a-weeping, and said, 'I perceive that God hath sent you to my house, and put it into your heart to go along with me, and permitted the Devil to appear visibly among us this night. I never saw the like before. Let me have the help of your prayers.' After this he became a singular Christian."

Mr. Peden was also somewhat of a prophet, and his speciality appears to have been the prognostication of unpleasant events, at all events to persons in Ireland. Two instances will suffice. When in a gentleman's house in co. Antrim he foretold that a maid-servant was *enceinte*, that she would murder the child, and would be punished. "Which accordingly came to pass, and she was burnt at Craig Fergus." On another occasion two messengers were sent to inform the Lord-Lieutenant that the Presbyterian ministers in Ireland should affirm that they had nothing to do with the rebellion at Bothwell Bridge. Mr.

Peden said they were on the Devil's errand, but God would arrest them by the gate. Accordingly one was stricken with sickness, while the other fell from his horse and broke his leg.

Footnotes

1. Furnished to the writer by T. J. Westropp, Esq., M.A.
2. Glanvill, *Sadducismus Triumphatus*, Rel. 26.
3. *Ulster Journal of Archæology*, vol. iii. (for 1855).
4. Glanvill, *op. cit.*, Rel. 27.
5. Law's *Memorialls*.
6. Baxter, *Certainty of the World of Spirits*.
7. William Turner, *Compleat History of Most Remarkable Providences* (London, 1697).
8. Seymour, *Succession of Clergy in Cashel and Emly*.
9. O'Donoghue, *Brendaniana*, p. 301. See Joyce, *Wonders of Ireland*, p. 30, for an apparition of a ship in the air in Celtic times. See also Westropp, *Brasil* (Proc. R.I.A.); that writer actually sketched an illusionary island in 1872.
10. *Memorialls*.
11. Glanvill, *op. cit.*, Rel. 18; Baxter, *op. cit.*
12. *Op. cit.*; W. P., *History of Witches and Wizards* (London, 1700 ?).
13. John Lindon (or Lyndon) became junior puisne judge of the Chief Place in 1682, was knighted in 1692, and died in 1697 (*Cork Hist. and Arch. Journal*, vol. vii., 2nd series).
14. Egmont MSS. (Hist. MSS. Comm.), ii. 181.

CHAPTER VII

A.D. 1688

AN IRISH-AMERICAN WITCH

IT is often said that Irishmen succeed best out of Ireland; those qualities they possess, which fail to ripen and come to maturity in the lethargic atmosphere of the Green Isle, where nothing matters very much provided public opinion is not run counter to, become factors of history under the sunshine and storm of countries where more ample scope is given for the full development of pugnacity, industry, or state-craft. At any rate, from the days of Duns Scotus and St. Columbanus down to the present, Irishmen have filled, and still fill, positions of the highest importance in every part of the globe as friends of kings, leaders of armies, or preachers of the Truth—of such every Irishman, be his creed or politics what they may, is justly proud. To the lengthy and varied list of honours and offices may be added (in one instance at least) the item of witchcraft. Had the unhappy creature, whose tale is related below, remained in her native land, she would most probably have ended her days in happy oblivion as a poor old woman, in no way distinguishable from hundreds of others in like position; as it was, she attained unenviable notoriety as a powerful witch, and was almost certainly the means of starting the outbreak at Salem. Incidentally the story is of interest as showing that at this time there were some Irish-speaking people in Boston.

Shortly after the date of its colonisation the State of Massachusetts became remarkable for its cases of witchcraft; several persons were tried, and some were hanged, for this crime. But at the time about which we are writing there was in Boston a distinguished family of puritanical ministers named Mather. The father, Increase Mather, is to be identified with the person of that name who was Commonwealth "minister of the Gospel" at Magherafelt in Ireland in 1656; his more famous son, Cotton, was a most firm believer in all the possibilities of witchcraft, and it is to his pen that we owe the following. He first gave an account of it to the world in his *Memorable Providences relating to Witchcraft*, published at Boston in 1689, the year after its occurrence; and subsequently reproduced it, though in a more condensed form, in his better-known *Magnalia Christi* (London, 1702). It is from this latter source that we have taken it, and the principal passages which are omitted in it, but occur in the *Memorable Providences*, are here inserted either within square brackets in the text, or as footnotes. We may now let the reverend gentleman tell his tale in his own quaint and rotund phraseology.

"Four children of John Goodwin in Boston which had enjoyed a Religious Education, and answer'd it with a towardly Ingenuity; Children indeed of an exemplary Temper and Carriage, and an Example to all about them for Piety, Honesty, and Industry. These were in the year 1688 arrested by a stupendous Witchcraft. The Eldest of the children, a Daughter of about Thirteen years old, saw fit to examine their Laundress, the Daughter of a Scandalous Irish Woman in the Neighbourhood, whose name was Glover [whose miserable husband before he died had sometimes complained of her, that she was undoubtedly a witch, and that wherever his head was laid, she would quickly arrive unto the punishments due to such a one], about Some Linnen that was missing, and the Woman bestowing very bad language on the Child, in the Daughter's Defence, the Child was immediately taken with odd Fits, that carried in them something Diabolical. It was not long before one of her Sisters, with two of her Brothers, were horribly taken with the like Fits, which the most Experienc'd Physicians [particularly our worthy and prudent friend Dr. Thomas Oakes] pronounced Extraordinary and preternatural;

and one thing the more confirmed them in this Opinion was, that all the Children were tormented still just the same part of their Bodies, at the same time, though their Pains flew like swift lightning from one part to another, and they were kept so far asunder that they neither saw nor heard each other's Complaints. At nine or ten a-clock at Night they still had a Release from their miseries, and slept all Night pretty comfortably. But when the Day came they were most miserably handled. Sometimes they were Deaf, sometimes Dumb, and sometimes Blind, and often all this at once. Their tongues would be drawn down their throats, and then pull'd out upon their Chins, to a prodigious Length. Their Mouths were forc'd open to such a Wideness, that their jaws were out of joint; and anon clap together again, with a Force like a Springlock: and the like would happen to their Shoulder-blades, their Elbows and Handwrists, and several of their joints . . . Their Necks would be broken, so that their Neck-bone would seem dissolv'd unto them that felt after it, and yet on the sudden it would become again so stiff, that there was no stirring of their Heads; yea, their Heads would be twisted almost round. And if the main Force of their Friends at any time obstructed a dangerous Motion which they seemed upon, they would roar exceedingly. "But the Magistrates being awakened by the Noise of these Grievous and Horrid Occurrences, examin'd the Person who was under the suspicion of having employ'd these Troublesome Dæmons, and she gave such a Wretched Account of herself that she was committed unto the Gaoler's Custody. [Goodwin had no proof that could have done her any hurt; but the hag had not power to deny her interest in the enchantment of the children; and when she was asked, Whether she believed there was a God? her answer was too blasphemous and horrible for any pen of mine to mention. Upon the commitment of this extraordinary woman all the children had some present ease, until one related to her, accidentally meeting one or two of them, entertain'd them with her blessing, that is railing, upon which three of them fell ill again.]

"It was not long before this Woman was brought upon her Trial; but then [thro' the efficacy of a charm, I suppose, used upon her by one or some of her crue] the Court could have no Answers from her but in the Irish, which was her Native Language, although she understood English very well, and had accustom'd her whole Family to none but English in her former Conversation. [It was long before she could with any direct answers plead unto her Indictment, and when she did plead] it was with owning and bragging rather than denial of her Guilt. And the Interpreters, by whom the Communication between the Bench and the Barr was managed, were made sensible that a Spell had been laid by another Witch on this, to prevent her telling Tales, by confining her to a language which 'twas hoped nobody would understand. The Woman's House being searched, several Images, or Poppets, or Babies, made of Raggs and stuffed with Goat's Hair, were found; when these were produced the vile Woman confess'd, that her way to torment the Objects of her Malice was by wetting of her Finger with her Spittle, and stroaking of these little Images. The abus'd Children were then produced in Court, and the Woman still kept stooping and shrinking, as one that was almost prest to death with a mighty Weight upon her. But one of the Images being brought to her, she odly and swiftly started up, and snatch'd it into her Hand. But she had no sooner snatch'd it than one of the Children fell into sad Fits before the whole Assembly. The judges had their just Apprehensions at this, and carefully causing. a repetition of the Experiment, they still found the same Event of it, tho' the Children saw not when the Hand of the Witch was laid upon the Images. They ask'd her, *Whether she had any to stand by her?* She reply'd, *She had*; and looking very fixtly into the air, she added, *No, he's gone!* and then acknowledged she had One, who was her Prince, with whom she mention'd I know not what Communion. For which cause the Night after she was heard expostulating with a Devil for his thus deserting her, telling him, that because he had served her so basely and falsely she had confessed all.

"However to make all clear the Court appointed five or six Physicians to examine her very strictly, whether she were no way craz'd in her Intellectuals. Divers Hours did they spend with her, and in all that while no Discourse came from her but what was agreeable; particularly when they ask'd her what she thought would become of her Soul, she reply'd, *You ask me a very solemn Question, and I cannot tell what to say to it.* She profest herself a Roman Catholick, and could recite her Paternoster in Latin very readily, but there was one Clause or two always too hard for her, whereof she said, *She could not repeat it, if she might have all the world.* [1] In the Upshot the Doctors returned her Compos Mentis, and Sentence of Death was past upon her.

"Divers Days past between her being arraign'd and condemn'd; and in this time, one Hughes testify'd, that her Neighbour (called Howen), who was cruelly bewitchd unto Death about six years before, laid her Death to the charge of this Woman [she had seen Glover sometimes come down her chimney], and bid her, the said Hughes, to remember this; for within six years there would be occasion to mention it. [This Hughes now preparing her testimony, immediately one of her children, a fine boy well grown towards youth] was presently taken ill in the same wofal manner that Goodwin's were; and particularly the Boy in the Night cry'd out, that a Black Person with a Blue Cap in the Room tortur'd him, and that they try'd with their Hand in the Bed for to pull out his Bowels. The Mother of the Boy went unto Glover on the day following, and asked her, *Why she tortured her poor Lad at such a rate?* Glover answered, *Because of the Wrong she had receiv'd from her,* and boasted *That she had come at him as a Black Person with a Blue Cap, and with her Hand in the Bed would have pulled his Bowels out, but could not.* Hughes denied that she had wronged her; and Glover then desiring to see the Boy, wished him well; upon which he had no more of his Indisposition.

"After the Condemnation of the Woman, I did my self give divers Visits to her, wherein she told me, that she did use to be at Meetings, where her Prince with Four more were present. She told me who the Four were, and plainly said, *That her Prince was the Devil.* [She entertained me with nothing but Irish, which language I had not learning enough to understand without an interpreter.] When I told her that, and how her Prince had deserted her, she reply'd [I think in English, and with passion too], *If it be so, I am sorry for that.* And when she declined answering some things that I ask'd her, she told me, *She could give me a full answer, but her Spirits would not give her leave: nor could she consent, she said, without this leave that I should pray for her.* [However against her will I pray'd with her, which if it were a fault it was in excess of pity. When I had done she thanked me with many good words, but I was no sooner out of her sight than she took a stone, a long and slender stone, and with her finger and spittle fell to tormenting it; though whom or what she meant I had the mercy never to understand.] At her Execution she said the afflicted Children should not be relieved by her Death, for others besides she had a hand in their Affliction."

Mrs. Glover was hanged, but in accordance with her dying words the young Goodwins experienced no relief from their torments, or, as Cotton Mather characteristically puts it, "the Three Children continued in their Furnace, as before; and it grew rather seven times hotter than before," and as this was brought about by our Irish witch it may not be out of place to give some extracts relative to the extraordinary adventures that befel them. In their Fits they cried out of *They* and *Them* as the Authors of all their Miseries; but who that *They* and *Them* were, they were not able to declare. Yet at last one of the Children was able to discern their Shapes, and utter their names. A Blow at the Place where they saw the Spectre was always felt by the Boy himself in that part of his Body that answer'd what might be stricken at. And this tho' his Back were turned, and the thing so done, that there could be no Collusion in it. But a Blow at the Spectre always helped him too, for he would have a respite from his Ails a considerable while, and the Spectre would be gone. Yea, 'twas very credibly affirmed, that a dangerous Woman or two in the Town received Wounds by the Blows thus given to their spectres... Sometimes they would be very mad, and then they would climb over high Fences, yea, they would fly like Geese, and be carry'd with an incredible

Swiftness through the Air, having but just their Toes now and then upon the Ground (sometimes not once in Twenty Foot), and their Arms wav'd like the Wings of a Bird . . . If they were bidden to do a *needless* thing (as to rub a *clean* Table) they were able to do it unmolested; but if to do any *useful* thing (as to rub a *dirty* Table), they would presently, with many Torments, be made incapable."

Finally Cotton Mather took the eldest of the three children, a girl, to his own house, partly out of compassion for her parents, but chiefly, as he tells us "that I might be a critical Eye-witness of things that would enable me to confute the Sadducism of this Debauched Age"—and certainly her antics should have provided him with a quiverful of arguments against the "Sadducees." "In her Fits she would cough up a Ball as big as a small Egg into the side of her Windpipe that would near choak her, till by Stroaking and by Drinking it was again carry'd down. When I pray'd in the Room her Hands were with a *strong*, though not *even*, Force clapt upon her Ears. And when her Hands were by our Force pull'd away, she cry'd out, *They make such a noise, I cannot hear a word*. She complained that Glover's chain was upon her Leg; and assaying to go, her Gate was exactly such as the chain'd Witch had before she dy'd. [Sometimes she imagined she was mounted on horseback], and setting herself in a riding Posture, she would in her Chair be agitated, as one sometimes Ambling, sometimes Trotting, and sometimes Galloping very furiously. In these Motions we could not perceive that she was mov'd by the Stress of her Feet upon the Ground, for often she touched it not. When she had rode a Minute or two, she would seem to be at a Rendezvous with Them that were her Company, and there she would maintain a Discourse with them, asking them many Questions concerning her self. At length she pretended that her Horse could ride up the Stairs; and unto admiration she rode (that is, was toss'd as one that rode) up the Stair."

Subsequently, when the clergy of Boston and Charleston had kept a day of prayer with fasting, the children improved until they became perfectly well. But in an unlucky moment Mr. Mather determined to entertain his congregation with a sermon on these *Memorable Providences*, and the study of this again affected the girl. Formerly, in the worst of her attacks, she had been most dutiful and respectful to Cotton Mather, "but now her whole Carriage to me was with a Sauciness which I am not us'd anywhere to be treated withal. She would knock at my Study door, affirming *that some one below would be glad to see me*, tho' there was none that ask'd for me. And when I chid her for telling what was false, her Answer was *that Mrs. Mather is always glad to see you*! Once when lying in a fit, as he that was praying was alluding to the Words of the Canaanitess, and saying, *Lord, have mercy on a Daughter vext with a Devil*, there came a big, but low, voice from her, in which the Spectators did not see her Mouth to move, *There's two or three of us.*"

Finally after three days of fasting and prayer the children were completely cured, but the storm thus raised was not easily allayed. The old woman seems, like many another of her years and sex, to have been of a choleric and crotchety disposition, while it is also quite within the bounds of possibility that she had become so infected with the popular superstition (and who could blame her!) that she actually believed herself to be capable of harming people by merely stroking dolls, or stones with her finger. That not uncommon form of mental torture employed, namely, the making her repeat the Lord's Prayer, all the time watching carefully for *lapsus linguæ*, and thence drawing deductions as to her being in league with the Devil, was particularly absurd in the case of such a person as Mrs. Glover, whose memory was confused by age. At any rate there are probably very few of us at the present day who would care to be forced to say in public either that Prayer or the Apostles'

Creed if we knew that our lives depended on absolute verbal accuracy, and that the slightest slip might mean death. It is possible, too, that some of the fits of Goodwin's children were due to conscious imposture; and certain it is, from a study of the whole case, that the deep-rooted belief of the self-opinionated Cotton Mather in the truth of such things, as well as the flattering his vanity received, contributed very largely to the success of the whole incident. Cotton Mather's account of the case was very highly praised by Mr. Baxter in his *Certainty of the World of Spirits*, and this so delighted Mr. Mather that he distributed the latter work throughout New England as being one that should convince the most obdurate "Sadducee." The result of this was speedily seen. Three years after the Boston incident a similar outbreak occurred amongst some young persons in the house of the Rev. Samuel Parris at Salem, then a small village about nineteen miles north-east of Boston. The contagion spread with appalling rapidity; numerous persons were brought to trial, of whom, in the space of sixteen months, nineteen (*twenty-five* according to Ashton) [2] were hanged, one of them being a clergyman, the Rev. George Burroughs, about one hundred and fifty were put in prison, and more than two hundred accused of witchcraft. Finally the Government put a stop to the trials, and released the accused in April 1693; Mr. Parris, in whose house the affair commenced, was dismissed from his cure, as being the "Beginner and Procurer of the sorest Afflictions," but, directly and indirectly, Mrs. Glover may be considered the first cause, for if the case of Goodwin's children, had not occurred at Boston it is more than probable the village of Salem would never have been plagued as it was.

Footnotes

1. "An experiment was made, whether she could recite the Lord's Prayer: and it was found that though clause after clause was most carefully repeated unto her, yet when she said it after them that prompted her, she could not possibly avoid making nonsense of it, with some ridiculous depravations. This experiment I had the curiosity to see made upon two more, and it had the same effect."
2. *The Devil in Britain and America*, chap. xxiv.

CHAPTER VIII

A.D. 1689-1720

PORTENT ON ENTRY OF JAMES II—
WITCHCRAFT IN CO. ANTRIM—TRADITIONAL
VERSION OF SAME—EVENTS PRECEDING THE
ISLAND-MAGEE WITCH-TRIAL,—THE TRIAL
ITSELF—DR. FRANCIS HUTCHINSON.

THE account of the following portent is given us in Aubrey's *Miscellanies*. "When King James II first entered Dublin after his Arrival from France, 1689, one of the Gentlemen that bore the Mace before him, stumbled without any rub in his way, or other visible occasion. The Mace fell out of his hands, and the little Cross upon the Crown thereof stuck fast between two Stones in the Street. This is well known all over Ireland, and did much trouble King James himself with many of his chief Attendants"; but no doubt greatly raised the hopes of his enemies.

A few years later a witch-story comes from the north of Ireland, and is related by George Sinclair in his *Satan's Invisible World displayed* (in later editions, not in the first). This book, by the way, seems to have been extremely popular, as it was reprinted several times, even as late as 1871. "At Antrim in Ireland a little girl of nineteen (nine?) years of age, inferior to none in the place for beauty, education, and birth, innocently put a leaf of sorrel which she had got from a witch into her mouth, after she had given the begging witch bread and beer at the door; it was scarce swallowed by her, but she began to be tortured in the bowels, to tremble all over, and even was convulsive, and in fine to swoon away as dead. The doctor used remedies on the 9th of May 1698, at which time it happened, but to no purpose, the child continued in a most terrible paroxysm; whereupon they sent for the minister, who scarce had laid his hand upon her when she was turned by the demon in the most dreadful shapes. She began first to rowl herself about, then to vomit needles, pins, hairs, feathers, bottoms of thread, pieces of glass, window-nails, nails drawn out of a cart or coach-wheel, an iron knife about a span long, eggs, and fish-shells and when the witch came near the place, or looked to the house, though at the distance of two hundred paces from where the child was, she was in worse torment, insomuch that no life was expected from the child till the witch was removed to some greater distance. The witch was apprehended, condemned, strangled, and burnt, and was desired to undo the incantation immediately before strangling; but said she could not, by reason others had done against her likewise. But the wretch confessed the same, with many more. The child was about the middle of September thereafter carried to a gentleman's house, where there were many other things scarce credible, but that several ministers and the gentleman have attested the same. The relation is to be seen in a pamphlet printed 1699, and entitled *The Bewitching of a Child in Ireland*."

Baxter in his *Certainty of the World of Spirits* quotes what at first sight appears to be the same case, but places it at Utrecht, and dates it 1625. But it is quite possible for a similar incident to have occurred on the Continent as well as in Ireland; many cases of witchcraft happening at widely different places and dates have points of close resemblance. Sinclair's story appears to be based on an actual trial for witchcraft in co. Antrim, the more so as he has drawn his information from a pamphlet on the subject which was printed the year after its occurrence. The mention of this latter is particularly interesting; it was probably locally printed, but there appears to be no means of tracing it, and indeed it must have been thumbed out of existence many years ago. The above story, marvellous though it may seem, is capable of explanation. The oxalic acid in sorrel is an irritant poison, causing retching and violent pains. But when once the suspicion of *witchcraft* arose the ejection of such an extraordinary collection of miscellaneous articles followed quite as a matter of course—it would, so to speak, have been altogether against the rules of the game for the girl to have got rid of anything else at that particular date.

Classon Porter gives what he considers to be the traditional version of the above.

According to it the supposed witch was a poor old woman, who was driven mad by the cruel and barbarous treatment which she received from many of her neighbours on the ground of her being a witch. To escape this treatment she sought refuge in a cave, which was in a field attached to the old (not the present) meeting-house in Antrim. Her living in such a place being thought a confirmation of what was alleged against her, she was thereupon stabbed to death, and her body cut in pieces, which were then scattered over the places where she was supposed to have exercised her evil influence. For some years after this terrible tragedy her ghost, in the form of a goat, was believed to haunt the session-house of the old meeting-house near which she had met her cruel fate; it was popularly known as MacGregor's ghost, this having been the name of the man who was sexton of the meeting-house when these things took place, and who probably had been concerned in the murder. So far Classon Porter. But we very much doubt if the above has really any connection with the Antrim witch-case of 1698. It seems more probable that it occurred at a later date, possibly after the Island-Magee trial, and thus would be an instance of one of those outbursts of cruelty on the part of a mob rendered ferocious by ignorance and superstition, of which examples are to be found in England during the eighteenth and nineteenth centuries.

On one occasion an Irish witch or wise woman was the means of having a Scotch girl delated by the Kirk for using charms at Hallow-Eve apparently for the purpose of discovering who her future husband should be. She confessed that "at the instigation of an old woman from Ireland she brought in a pint of water from a well which brides and burials pass over, and dipt her shirt into it, and hung it before the fire; that she either dreamed, or else there came something and turned about the chair on which her shirt was, but she could not well see what it was." Her sentence was a rebuke before the congregation; considering the state of Scotland at that period it must be admitted she escaped very well. [1]

We now come to the last instance of witches being tried and convicted in Ireland—as offenders against the laws of the realm—the celebrated Island-Magee case. There is a very scarce published account of this, said to have been compiled by an eyewitness, and entitled: "A Narrative of the sufferings of a young girl called Mary Dunbar, who was strangely molested by spirits and witches, at Mr. James Haltridge's house, parish of Island Magee, near Carrigfergus, in the County of Antrim, and Province of Ulster, in Ireland, and in some other places to which she was removed during her disorder; as also of the aforesaid Mr. Haltridge's house being haunted by spirits in the latter end of 1710 and beginning of 1711." This continued for many years in manuscript, but in 1822 it was printed as a pamphlet at Belfast, under the editorship of M'Skimin, author of the *History of Carrigfergus*. This pamphlet we have not seen; but full particulars of the entire case can be obtained by combining the following sources of information, viz. Wright's *Narratives of Sorcery and Witchcraft*; the *Dublin University Magazine*, vol. lxxxii.; a letter by Dr. Tisdall, the Vicar of Belfast, in the *Hibernian Magazine* for January 1775; Classon Porter's pamphlet; M'Skimin's *History of Carrigfergus* (ed. M'Crum, 1909); while the depositions that were taken are published in Young's *Historical Notices of Old Belfast*, pp. 161-4.

The actual trial of the witches was preceded by a series of most extraordinary incidents. In September 1710, Mrs. Anne Haltridge, widow of the Rev. John Haltridge, late Presbyterian minister at Island Magee, while staying in the house of her son, James Haltridge of the same place, suffered great annoyance every night from some invisible object, which threw stones and turf at her bed, the force of the blow often causing the curtains to open, and even drawing them from one end of the bed to the other. About the same time, also, the pillows were taken from under her head, and the clothes pulled off; and though a strict search was made, nothing could be discovered. Continuing to be annoyed in this way she removed to another room, being afraid to remain in her own any longer.

Then about the 11th of December, as she was sitting in the twilight at the kitchen fire, a little boy came in and sat down beside her. He appeared to be about eleven or twelve years old, with short black hair, having an old black bonnet on his head, a half-worn blanket about him trailing on the floor, and a torn vest under it, and kept his face covered with the blanket held before it. Mrs. Haltridge asked him several questions: Where he came from? Where he was going? Was he cold or hungry? and so on; but instead of answering her he got up and danced very nimbly round the kitchen, and then ran out of the house and disappeared in the cow-shed. The servants ran after him, but he was nowhere to be seen; when they returned to the house, however, there he was beside them. They tried to catch him, but every time they attempted it he ran off and could not be found. At last one of the servants, seeing the master's dog coming in, cried out that her master was returning home, and that he would soon catch the troublesome creature, upon which he immediately vanished, nor were they troubled with him again till February 1711.

On the 11th of that month, which happened to be a Sunday, old Mrs. Haltridge was reading Dr. Wedderburn's *Sermons on the Covenant*, when, laying the book aside for a little while, nobody being in the room all the time, it was suddenly taken away. She looked for it everywhere, but could not find it. On the following day the apparition already referred to came to the house, and breaking a pane of glass in one of the windows, thrust in his hand with the missing volume in it. He began to talk with one of the servants, Margaret Spear, and told her that he had taken the book when everybody was down in the kitchen, and that her mistress would never get it again. The girl asked him if he could read it, to which he replied that he could, adding that the Devil had taught him. Upon hearing this extraordinary confession she exclaimed, "The Lord bless me from thee! Thou hast got ill lear (learning)." He told her she might bless herself as often as she liked, but that it could not save her; whereupon he produced a sword, and threatened to kill everybody in the house. This frightened her so much that she ran into the parlour and fastened the door, but the apparition laughed at her, and declared that he could come in by the smallest hole in the house like a cat or mouse, as the Devil could make him anything he pleased. He then took up a large stone, and hurled it through the parlour window, which, upon trial, could not be put out at the same place. A little after the servant and child looked out, and saw the apparition catching the turkey-cock, which he threw over his shoulder, holding him by the tail; and the bird making a great sputter with his feet, the stolen book was spurred out of the loop in the blanket where the boy had put it. He then leaped over a wall with the turkey-cock on his back. Presently the girl saw him endeavouring to draw his sword to kill the bird, but it escaped. Missing the book out of his blanket he ran nimbly up and down in search of it, and then with a club came and broke the glass of the parlour window. The girl again peeped out through the kitchen window, and saw him digging with his sword. She summoned up courage to ask him what he was doing, and he answered, "Making a grave for a corpse which will come out of this house very soon." He refused, however, to say who it would be, but having delivered himself of this enlivening piece of information, flew over the hedge as if he had been a bird.

For a day or two following nothing happened, but on the morning of the 15th the clothes were mysteriously taken off Mrs. Haltridge's bed, and laid in a bundle behind it. Being put back by some of the family they were again removed, and this time folded up and placed under a large table which happened to be in the room. Again they were laid in order on the bed, and again they were taken off, and this. third time made up in the shape of a corpse, or something that very closely resembled it. When this strange news spread through the neighbourhood many persons came to the house, and, after a thorough investigation lest there might be a trick in the matter, were obliged to acknowledge that there was some invisible agent at work. Mr. Robert Sinclair, the Presbyterian minister of the place, with John Man and Reynold Leaths, two of his Elders, stayed the whole of that day and the following night with the distressed family, spending much of the time in prayer. At night Mrs. Haltridge went to bed as usual in the haunted room, but got very little rest, and at about twelve o'clock she cried out suddenly as if in great pain. Upon Mr. Sinclair asking her what was the matter, she said she felt as if a knife had been stuck into her back. Next morning she quitted the haunted room and went to another; but the violent pain never left her back, and at the end of the week, on the 22nd of February, she died. During her illness the clothes were frequently taken off the bed which she occupied, and made up like a corpse, and even when a table and chairs were laid upon them to keep them on, they were mysteriously removed without any noise, and made up as before; but this never happened when anyone was in the room.

The evening before she died they were taken off as usual; but this time, instead of being made up in the customary way, they were folded with great care, and laid in a chest upstairs, where they were only found after a great deal of searching.

We now reach the account of the witchcraft proper, and the consequent trial. In or about the 27th of February 1711, a girl about eighteen years of age, Miss Mary Dunbar, whom Dr. Tisdall describes as "having an open and innocent countenance, and being a very intelligent young person," came to stay with Mrs. Haltridge, junior, to keep her company after her mother-in-law's death. A rumour was afloat that the latter had been bewitched into her grave, and this could not fail to have its effect on Miss Dunbar. Accordingly on the night of her arrival her troubles began. When she retired to her bedroom, accompanied by another girl, they were surprised to find that a new mantle and some other wearing apparel had been taken out of a trunk and scattered through the house. Going to look for the missing articles, they found lying on the parlour floor an apron which two days before had been locked up in another apartment. This apron, when they found it, was rolled up tight, and tied fast with a string of its own material, which had upon it five strange knots 2 (Tisdall 3 says nine). These she proceeded to unloose, and having done so, she found a flannel cap, which had belonged to old Mrs. Haltridge, wrapped up in the middle of the apron. When she saw this she was frightened, and threw both cap and apron to young Mrs. Haltridge, who also was alarmed, thinking that the mysterious knots boded evil to some inmate of the house. That evening Miss Dunbar was seized with a most violent fit, and, recovering, cried out that a knife was run through her thigh, and that she was most grievously afflicted by three women, whom she described particularly, but did not then give any account of their names. About midnight she was, seized with a second fit; when she saw in her vision seven or eight women who conversed together, and in their conversation called each other by their names. When she came out of her fit she gave their names as Janet Liston, Elizabeth Cellor, Kate M'Calmont, Janet Carson, Janet Mean, Latimer, and one whom they termed Mrs. Ann. She gave so minute a description of them that several of them were guessed at, and sent from different parts of the district to the "Afflicted," as Dr. Tisdall terms her, whom she distinguished from many other women that were brought with them. "She was constantly more afflicted as they approached the house; particularly there was one Latimer, who had been sent from Carrigfergus privately by Mr. Adair, the dissenting teacher; who, when she came to the house where the Afflicted was, viz. in Island Magee, none of them suspected her, but the Afflicted fell into a fit as she came near the house, and recovering when the woman was in the chamber the first words she said were, *O Latimer, Latimer* (which was her name), and her description agreed most exactly to the person. After this manner were all the rest discovered; and at one time she singled out one of her tormentors amongst thirty whom they brought in to see if they could deceive her either in the name or description of the accused person. All this was sworn to by persons that were present, as having heard it from the Afflicted as she recovered from her several fits."

Between the 3rd and the 24th of March depositions relative to various aspects of the case were sworn to by several people, and the Mayor of Carrigfergus issued a warrant for the arrest of all suspected persons. Seven women were arrested; their names were

>Janet Mean, of Braid Island.
>Jane Latimer, of Irish quarter, Carrigfergus.
>Margaret Mitchell, of Kilroot.
>Catherine M'Calmont, of Island Magee.
>Janet Liston, *alias* Sellar, of same.
>Elizabeth Sellar, of same.
>Janet Carson, of same.

Her worst tormentors seem to have been taken into custody at an early stage in the proceedings, for Miss Dunbar stated in her deposition, made on the 12th of March, that since their arrest she received no annoyance, except from "Mrs. Ann, and another woman blind of an eye, who told her when Mr. Robb, the curate, was going to pray with and for her, that she should be little the better for his prayers, for they would hinder her from hearing them, which they accordingly did." In one of her attacks Miss Dunbar was informed by this "Mrs. Ann" that she should never be discovered by her name, as the rest had been, but she seems to have overlooked the fact that her victim was quite capable of giving an accurate *description* of her, which she accordingly did, and thus was the means of bringing about the apprehension of one Margaret Mitchell, upon which she became free from all annoyance, except that she felt something strange in her stomach which she would be glad to get rid of—and did, as we shall see presently.

With regard to the woman blind in one eye, we learn from another deponent that three women thus disfigured were brought to her, but she declared that they never troubled her. "One Jane Miller, of Carrigfergus, blind of an eye, being sent for, as soon as she drew near the house the said Mary, who did not know of her coming, became very much afraid, faintish, and sweat, and as soon as she came into the room the said Mary fell into such a violent fit of pains that three men were scarce able to bold her, and cryed out, 'For Christ's sake, take the Devil out of the room.' And being asked, said the third woman, for she was the woman that did torment her." Yet Jane Miller does not seem to have been arrested.

In one of the earliest of the depositions, that sworn by James Hill on the 5th of March, we find an extraordinary incident recorded, which seems to show that at least one of the accused was a victim of religious mania. He states that on the 1st of March, "he being in the house of William Sellar of Island Magee, one Mary Twmain (*sic!*) came to the said house and called out Janet Liston to speak to her, and that after the said Janet came in again she fell a-trembling, and told this Deponent that the said Mary had been desiring her to go to Mr. Haltridge's to see Mary Dunbar, but she declared she would not go for all Island Magee, except Mr. Sinclair would come for her, and said: If the plague of God was on her (Mary Dunbar), the plague of God be on them altogether; the Devil be with them if he was among them. If God had taken her health from her, God give her health: if the Devil had taken it from her, the Devil give it her. And then added: O misbelieving ones, eating and drinking damnation to themselves, crucifying Christ afresh, and taking all out of the hands of the Devil!"

Finally the accused were brought up for trial at Carrigfergus before Judges Upton and Macartney [4] on 31st March 1711. Amongst the witnesses examined were Mr. Skeffington, curate of Larne; Mr. Ogilvie, Presbyterian minister of Larne; Mr. Adair, Presbyterian minister of Carrigfergus; Mr. Cobham, Presbyterian minister of Broad Island; Mr. Edmonstone, of Red Hall, and others. The proceedings commenced at six o'clock in the morning, and lasted until two in the afternoon. An abstract of the evidence was made by Dr. Tisdall, who was present in Court during the trial, and from whose letter we extract the following passages—many of the foregoing facts (!) being also adduced.

"It was sworn to by most of the evidences that in some of her fits three strong men were scarce able to hold her down, that she would mutter to herself, and speak some words distinctly, and tell everything she had said in her conversation with the witches, and how she came to say such things, which she spoke when in her fits."

"In her fits she often had her tongue thrust into her windpipe in such a manner that she was like to choak, and the root seemed pulled up into her mouth. Upon her recovery she complained extremely of one Mean, who had twisted her tongue; and told the Court that she had tore her throat, and tortured her violently by reason of her crooked fingers and swelled knuckles. The woman was called to the Bar upon this evidence, and ordered to show her hand; it was really amazing to see the exact agreement betwixt the description of the Afflicted and the hand of the supposed tormentor; all the joints were distorted and the tendons shrivelled up, as she had described."

"One of the men who had held her in a fit swore she had nothing visible on her arms when he took hold of them, and that all in the room saw some worsted yarn tied round her wrist, which was put on invisibly; there were upon this string seven double knots and one single one. In another fit she cried out that she was grievously tormented with a pain about her knee; upon which the women in the room looked at her knee, and found a fillet tied fast about it; her mother swore to the fillet, that it was the same she had given her that morning, and had seen it about her head; this had also seven double knots and one single one."

"Her mother was advised by a Roman Catholic priest to use a countercharm, which was to write some words out of the first chapter of St. John's Gospel in a paper, and to tie the paper with an incle three times round her neck, knotted each time. This charm the girl herself declined; but the mother, in one of the times of her being afflicted, used it. She was in a violent fit upon the bed held down by a man, and, recovering a little, complained grievously of a pain in her back and about her middle; immediately the company discovered the said incle tied round her middle with seven double knots and one single one: this was sworn to by several. The man who held the Afflicted was asked by the judge if it were possible she could reach the incle about her neck while he held her; he said it was not, by the virtue of his oath, he having her hands fast down."

"The Afflicted, during one of her fits, was observed by several persons to slide off the bed in an unaccountable manner, and to be laid gently on the ground as if supported and drawn invisibly. Upon her recovery she told them the several persons who had drawn her in that manner, with the intention, as they told her, of bearing her out of the window; but that she reflecting at that time, and calling upon God in her mind, they let her drop on the floor."

"The Afflicted, recovering from a fit, told the persons present that her tormentors had declared that she should not have power to go over the threshold of the chamber-door; the evidence declared that they had several times attempted to lead her out of the door, and that she was as often thrown into fits as they had brought her to the said threshold; that to pursue the experiment further they had the said threshold taken up, upon which they were immediately struck with so strong a smell of brimstone that they were scarce able to bear it; that the stench spread through the whole house, and afflicted several to that degree that they fell sick in their stomachs, and were much disordered." The above were the principal facts sworn to in the Court, to which most of the witnesses gave their joint testimony.

"There was a great quantity of things produced in Court, and sworn to be what she vomited out of her throat. I had them all in my hand, and found there was a great quantity of feathers, cotton, yarn, pins, and two large waistcoat buttons, at least as much as would fill my hand. They gave evidence to the Court they had seen those very things coming out of her mouth, and had received them into their hands as she threw them up."

Her tormentors had told Miss Dunbar that she should have no power to give evidence against them in Court. "She was accordingly that day before the trial struck dumb, and so continued in Court during the whole trial, but had no violent fit. I saw her in Court cast her eyes about in a wild distracted manner.) and it was then thought she was recovering from her fit [of dumbness], and it was hoped she would give her own evidence. I observed, as they were raising her up, she sank into the arms of a person who held her, closed her eyes, and seemed perfectly senseless and motionless. I went to see her after the trial; she told me she knew not where she was when in Court; that she had been afflicted all that time by three persons, of whom she gave a particular description both of their proportion, habits, hair, features, and complexion, and said she had never seen them till the day before the trial."

The prisoners had no lawyer to defend them, while it is hardly necessary to say that no medical evidence as to the state of health of Miss Dunbar was heard. When the witnesses had been examined the accused were ordered to make their defence. They all positively denied the charge of witchcraft; one with the worst looks, who was therefore the greatest suspect, called God to witness that she was wronged. Their characters were inquired into, and some were reported unfavourably of, which seemed to be rather due to their ill appearance than to any facts proved against them. "It was made appear on oath that most of them had received the Communion, some of them very lately, that several of them had been laborious, industrious people, and had frequently been known to pray with their families, both publickly and privately; most of them could say the Lord's Prayer, which it is generally said they learnt in prison, they being every one Presbyterians."

"Judge Upton summed up the whole evidence with great exactness and perspicuity, notwithstanding the confused manner in which it was offered. He seemed entirely of opinion that the jury could not bring them in guilty upon the sole testimony of the afflicted person's visionary images. He said he could not doubt but that the whole matter was preternatural and diabolical, but he conceived that. had the persons accused been really witches and in compact with the Devil, it could hardly be presumed that they should be such constant attenders upon Divine Service, both in public and private."

Unfortunately his Brother on the Bench was not so open-minded. Judge Macartney, who is almost certainly the Counsel for the plaintiff in the Lostin case, differed altogether from him, and thought that the jury might well bring them in guilty.

The twelve good men and true lost no time in doing so, and, in accordance with the Statute, the prisoners were sentenced to a year's imprisonment, and to stand in the pillory four times during that period. It is said that when placed in this relic of barbarism the unfortunate wretches were pelted by the mob with eggs and cabbage-stalks to such an extent that one of them had an eye knocked out. And thus ended the last trial for witchcraft in Ireland.

It is significant that witch-trials stopped in all three countries within a decade of each other. The last condemnation in England occurred in 1712, when a woman in Hertfordshire, Jane Wenharn, was found guilty by a jury, but was reprieved at the representation of the judge; another trial occurred in 1717, but the accused were acquitted. In Scotland the Sheriff-depute of Sutherland passed sentence of death on a woman (though apparently illegally) in 1722, who was consequently strangled and burnt. Ashton indeed states (p. 192) that the last execution in Ireland occurred at Glarus, when a servant was burnt as a witch in 1786. This would be extremely interesting, were it not for the fact that it is utterly incorrect. It is clear from what J. Français says that this happened at Glaris *in Switzerland*, and was the last instance of judicial condemnation and execution in Europe. We have drawn attention to this lest it should mislead others, as it did us.

Before concluding this chapter it will not be out of place to mention the fact that one of the most strenuous writers against witchcraft subsequently ornamented the Irish Episcopal Bench. This was Dr. Francis Hutchinson, who wrote the "Historical Essay concerning Witchcraft" in the form of a dialogue between a clergyman (the author), a Scotch advocate, and an English juror. The first edition was published in 1718, and was followed by a second in 1720, in which year he was promoted to the See of Down and Connor. As to the value of his book, and the important position it occupied in the literary history of witchcraft in England, we cannot do better than quote Dr. Notestein's laudatory criticism. He says: "Hutchinson's book must rank with Reginald Scot's *Discoverie* as one of the great classics of English witch-literature. So nearly was his point of view that of our own day that it would be idle to rehearse his arguments. A man with warm sympathies for the oppressed, he had been led probably by the case of Jane Wenham, with whom he had talked, to make a personal investigation of all cases that came at all within the ken of those living. Whoever shall write the final story of English witchcraft will find himself still dependent upon this eighteenth-century historian. His work was the last chapter in the witch controversy. There was nothing more to say."

Footnotes

1. C. K. Sharpe, *op. cit.*
2. A man in the Orkneys was ruined by nine knots tied in a blue thread (Dalyell's *Darker Superstitions of Scotland*).
3. The Rev. Dr. Tisdall, who has given such a full account of the trial, was Vicar of Belfast. For his attitude towards the Presbyterians, see Witherow's *Memorials of Presbyterianism in Ireland*, pp. 118, 159. Yet his narrative of the trial is not biassed, for all his statements can be home out by other evidence.
4. James Macartney became second puisne justice of the King's Bench in 1701, puisne justice of Common Pleas (vice A. Upton) in 1714, and retired in 1726. Anthony Upton became puisne Justice of Common Pleas, was succeeded as above, and committed suicide in 1718. Both were natives of co. Antrim.

CHAPTER IX

A.D. 1807 TO PRESENT DAY

MARY BUTTERS, THE CARNMONEY WITCH—
BALLAD ON HER—THE HAND OF GLORY—A
JOURNEY THROUGH THE AIR—A "WITCH"
IN 1911—SOME MODERN ILLUSTRATIONS OF
CATTLE- AND MILK-MAGIC—TRANSFERENCE
OF DISEASE BY A cailleach—BURYING THE.
SHEAF—J.P.'S COMMISSION—CONCLUSION

OLD beliefs die hard, especially when their speedy demise is a consummation devoutly to be wished; if the Island-Magee case was the last instance of judicial condemnation of witchcraft as an offence against the laws of the realm it was very far indeed from being the last occasion on which a witch and her doings formed the centre of attraction in an Irish law-court. Almost a century after the Island-Magee incident the town of Carrigfergus again became the scene of action, when the celebrated "Carnmoney witch," Mary Butters, was put forward for trial at the Spring Assizes in March 1808. It is an instance of black magic versus white (if we may dignify the affair with the title of *magic*!), though it should be borne in mind that in the persecution of witches many women were put to death on the latter charge, albeit they were really benefactors of the human race; the more so as their skill in simples and knowledge of the medicinal virtue of herbs must have added in no small degree to, the resources of our present pharmacopœia. The following account of this is taken from the *Belfast News-Letter* for 21st August 1807, as well as from some notes by M'Skimin in Young's *Historical Notice of Old Belfast*.

One Tuesday night (evidently in August 1807) an extraordinary affair took place in the house of a tailor named Alexander Montgomery, who lived hard by Carnmoney Meeting-House. The tailor had a cow which continued to give milk as usual, but of late no butter could be produced from it. An opinion was unfortunately instilled into the mind of Montgomery's wife, that whenever such a thing occurred, it was occasioned by the cow having been bewitched. Her belief in this was strengthened by the fact that every old woman in the parish was able to relate some story illustrative of what she had seen or heard of in times gone by with respect to the same. At length the family were informed of a woman named Mary Butters, who resided at Carrigfergus. They went to her, and brought her to the house for the purpose of curing the cow. About ten o'clock that night war was declared against the unknown magicians. Mary Butters ordered old Montgomery and a young man named Carnaghan to go out to the cow-house, turn their waistcoats inside out, and in that dress to stand by the head of the cow until she sent for them, while the wife, the son, and an old woman named Margaret Lee remained in the house with her.

Montgomery and his ally kept their lonely vigil until daybreak, when, becoming alarmed at receiving no summons, they left their post and knocked at the door, but obtained no response. They then looked through the kitchen window, and to their horror saw the four inmates stretched on the floor as dead. They immediately burst in the door, and found that the wife and son were actually dead, and the sorceress and Margaret Lee nearly so. The latter soon afterwards expired; Mary Butters was thrown out on a dung-heap, and a restorative administered to her in the shape of a few hearty kicks, which had the desired effect. The house had a sulphureous smell, and on the fire was a large pot in which were milk, needles, pins, and crooked nails. At the inquest held at Carnmoney on the 19th of August, the jurors stated that the three victims had come by their deaths from suffocation, owing to Mary Butters having made use of some noxious ingredients, after the manner of a charm, to recover a sick cow. She was brought up at the Assizes, but was discharged by proclamation. Her version of the story was, that a black man had appeared in the house armed with a huge club, with which he killed the three persons and stunned herself.

Lamentable though the whole affair was, as well for the gross superstition displayed by the participants as for its tragical ending, yet it seems to have aroused no other feelings amongst the inhabitants of Carnmoney and Carrigfergus than those of risibility and derision. A clever racy ballad was made upon it by a resident in the district, which, as it is probably the only poem on the subject of witchcraft in Ireland, we print here in its entirety from the *Ulster Journal of Archæology* for 1908, though we have not had the courage to attempt a glossary to the "braid Scots." It adds some picturesque details to the more prosaic account of the *News-Letter*.

"In Carrick town a wife did dwell
    Who does pretend to conjure witches.
Auld Barbara Goats, or Lucky Bell,
    Ye'll no lang to come through her clutches,
A waeful trick this wife did play
    On simple Sawney, our poor tailor.
She's mittimiss'd the other day
    To lie in limbo with the jailor.
This simple Sawney had a cow,
    Was aye as sleekit as an otter;
It happened for a month or two
    Aye when they churn'd they got nae butter,
Rown-tree tied in the cow's tail,

  And vervain glean'd about the ditches;
 These freets and charms did not prevail,
  They could not banish the auld witches.
The neighbour wives a' gathered in
  In number near about a dozen;
Elspie Dough, and Mary Linn,
  An' Kate M'Cart, the tailor's cousin.
Aye they churn'd and aye they swat,
  Their aprons loos'd, and coost their mutches
But yet nae butter they could get,
  They blessed the cow but curst the witches.
Had Sawney summoned all his wits
  And sent awa for Huie Mertin,
He could have gall'd the witches' guts,
  An' cur't the kye to Nannie Barton. [1]
But he may shew the farmer's wab,
  An' lang wade through Carnmoney gutters;
Alas! it was a sore mis-jab
  When he employ'd auld Mary Butters.
The sorcerest open'd the scene
  With magic words of her invention,
To make the foolish people keen
  Who did not know her base intention,
She drew a circle round the churn,
  And washed the staff in south-run water, [2]
And swore the witches she would burn,
  But she would have the tailor's butter.
When sable Night her curtain spread
  Then she got on a flaming fire;
The tailor stood at the cow's head
  With his turn'd waistcoats [3] in the byre.

The chimney covered with a scraw
    An' every crevice where it smoak'd,
But long before the cock did craw
    The people in the house were choak'd.
The muckle pot hung on all night,
    As Mary Butters had been brewing
In hopes to fetch some witch or wight,
    Whas entrails by her art were stewing.
In this her magic a' did fail;
    Nae witch nor wizard was detected.
Now Mary Butters lies in jail
    For the base part that she has acted.
The tailor lost his son and wife,
    For Mary Butters did them smother;
But as he hates a single life
    In four weeks' time he got another.
He is a crouse auld canty chiel,
    An' cares nae what the witches mutter
He'll never mair employ the Deil,
    Nor his auld agent Mary Butters.
At day the tailor left his post
    Though he had seen no apparition,
Nae wizard grim, nae witch, nor ghost,
    Though still he had a stray suspicion
That some auld wizard wrinkled wife
    Had cast her cantrips o'er poor brawney
Cause she and he did live in strife,
    An' whar's the man can blame poor Sawney.
Wae sucks for our young lasses now,
    For who can read their mystic matters,
Or tell if their sweethearts be true,
    The folks a' run to Mary Butters.

> To tell what thief a horse did steal,
>   In this she was a mere pretender,
> An' has nae art to raise the Deil
>   Like that auld wife, the Witch of Endor.
> If Mary Butters be a witch
>   Why but the people all should know it,
> An' if she can the muses touch
>   I'm sure she'll soon descry the poet.
> Her ain familiar aff she'll sen'
>   Or paughlet wi' a tu' commission
> To pour her vengeance on the man
>   That tantalizes her condition."

There also exists a shorter version of the ballad, which seems to be a rather clumsy adaptation of what we have given above; in it the witch is incorrectly termed *Butlers*. That the heroine did not evolve the procedure she had adopted out of her own fervent imagination, but that she followed a method generally recognised and practised in the country-side is shown by a case that occurred at Newtownards in January 1871.[4] A farm-hand had brought an action against his employer for wages alleged to be due to him. It transpired in the course of the evidence that on one occasion he had been set to banish witches that were troubling the cows. His method of working illustrates the Carnmoney case. All left the house except the plaintiff, who locked himself in, closed the windows, stopped all keyholes and apertures, and put sods on top of the chimneys. He then placed a large pot of sweet milk on the fire, into which he threw three rows of pins that had never been used, and three packages of needles; all were allowed to boil together for half an hour, and, as there was no outlet for the smoke, the plaintiff narrowly escaped being suffocated.

It is strange to find use made in Ireland of that potent magical instrument, the Hand of Glory, and that too in the nineteenth century. On the night of the 3rd of January 1831, some Irish thieves attempted to commit a robbery on the estate of Mr. Naper, of Loughcrew, co. Meath. They entered the house, armed with a dead man's hand with a lighted candle in it, believing in the superstitious notion that if such a hand be procured, and a candle placed within its grasp, the latter cannot be seen by anyone except him by whom it is used; also that if the candle and hand be introduced into a house it will prevent those who may be asleep from awaking. The inhabitants, however, were alarmed, and the robbers fled, leaving the hand behind them. [5] No doubt the absolute failure of this gruesome dark lantern on this occasion was due to the fact that neither candle nor candlestick had been properly prepared! The orthodox recipe for its preparation and consequent effectual working may be found in full in Mr. Baring Gould's essay on Schamir in his *Curious Myths of the Middle Ages*.

The following tale comes from an article in the *Dublin University Magazine*, vol. lxiv.; it has rather a Cross-Channel appearance, but may have been picked up locally in Ireland. A man named Shamus Rua (Red James) was awakened one night by a noise in the kitchen. He stole down, and found his old housekeeper, Madge, with half a dozen of her kidney, sitting by the fire drinking his whisky. When the bottle was finished one of them cried, "It's time to be off," and at the same moment she put on a peculiar red cap, and added

"By yarrow and rue,
And my red cap, too,
Hie over to England!"

And seizing a twig she soared up the chimney, whither she was followed by all save Madge. As the latter was making her preparations Shamus rushed into the kitchen, snatched the cap from her, and placing himself astride of her twig uttered the magic formula. He speedily found himself high in the air over the Irish Sea, and swooping through the empyrean at a rate unequalled by the fastest aeroplane. They rapidly neared the Welsh coast, and espied a castle afar off, towards the door of which they rushed with frightful velocity; Shamus closed his eyes and awaited the shock, but found to his delight that he had slipped through the keyhole without hurt. The party made their way to the cellar, where they caroused heartily, but the wine proved too heady, and somehow Shamus was captured and dragged before the lord of the castle, who sentenced him to be hanged. On his way to the gallows an old woman in the crowd called out in Irish "Ah, Shamus *alanna*! Is it going to die you are in a strange place without your little red cap?" He craved, and obtained, permission to put it on. On reaching the place of execution he was allowed to address the spectators, and did so in the usual ready-made speech, beginning,

"Good people all, a warning take by me."

But when he reached the last line,

"My parents reared me tenderly"

instead of stopping be unexpectedly added,

"By yarrow and rue," &c.,

with the result that he shot up through the air, to the great dismay of all beholders.

Our readers will at once recall Grandpapa's Tale of the Witches' Frolic in the *Ingoldsby Legends*. Similar tales appear in Scotland, for which see Sharpe, pp. 56, 207; the same writer (p. 212) makes mention of a red cap being worn by a witch.

After the opening years of the eighteenth century, when once it had ceased to attract the unwelcome attentions of judge, jury, and executioner, witchcraft degenerated rapidly. It is said by some writers that a belief in the old-fashioned witch of history may still be found in the remoter parts of rural England; the same can hardly be said of Ireland, this being due to the fact that witchcraft was never, at its best (or worst) period, very prevalent in this country. But its place is taken by an ineradicable belief in *pishogues*, or in the semi-magical powers of the bone-setter, or the stopping of bleeding wounds by an incantation, or the healing of diseases in human beings or animals by processes unknown to the medical profession, or in many other quaint tenets which lie on the borderland between folklore and witchcraft, and at best only represent the complete degeneracy and decay of the latter. Yet these practices sometimes come, for one reason or another, within the wide reach of the arm of the law, though it is perhaps unnecessary to state that they are not treated as infringements of the Elizabethan Statute. For example, some years ago a case was tried at New Pallas in co. Limerick, where a woman believed that another desired to steal her butter by *pishogues*, flew in a passion, assaulted her and threw her down, breaking her arm in the fall. [6] That appalling tragedy, the "witch-burning" case that occurred near Clonmel in 1895, is altogether misnamed. The woman was burnt, not because she was a witch, but in the belief that the real wife had been taken away and a fairy changeling substituted in her place; when the latter was subjected to the fire it would disappear, and the wife would be restored. Thus the underlying motive was kindness, but oh, how terribly mistaken! Lefanu in his *Seventy Years of Irish Life* relates a similar incident, but one which fortunately ended humorously rather than tragically: while Crofton Croker mentions instances of wives being taken by the fairies, and restored to their husbands after the lapse of years.

Even as late as the summer of 1911 the word "witch" was heard in an Irish law-court, when an unhappy poor woman was tried for killing another, an old-age pensioner, in a fit of insanity. [7] One of the witnesses deposed that he met the accused on the road on the morning of the murder. She had a statue in her hand, and repeated three times: "I have the old witch killed I got power from the Blessed Virgin to kill her. She came to me at 3 o'clock yesterday, and told me to kill her, or I would be plagued with rats and mice." She made much the same statement to another witness, and added: "We will be all happy now. I have the devils hunted away. They went across the hill at 3 o'clock yesterday." The evidence having concluded, the accused made a statement which was reduced to writing: "On the day of the thunder and lightning and big rain there did a rat come into my house, and since then I was annoyed and upset in my mind . . . A lady came to me when I was lying in bed at night, she was dressed in white, with a wreath on her head, and said that I was in danger. I thought that she was referring to the rat coming into the house . . . The lady who appeared to me said, If you receive this old woman's pension-book without taking off her clothes and cleaning them, and putting out her bed and cleaning up the house, you will receive dirt for ever, and rats and mice."

Imagine the above occurring in 1611 instead of 1911! The ravings of the poor demented creature would be accepted as gospel-truth; the rat would be the familiar sent by the witch to torment her, the witnesses would have many more facts to add to their evidence, the credulous people would rejoice that the country-side had been freed from such a malignant witch (though they might regret that she had been given her *congé* so easily), while the annals of Irish witchcraft would be the richer by nearly as extraordinary a case as that of Florence Newton, and one which would have lost nothing in the telling or the printing. Shorn of their pomp and circumstance, no doubt many witch-stories would be found to be very similar in origin to the above.

As is only to be expected in a country where the majority of the inhabitants are engaged in agricultural pursuits, most of the tales of strange doings are in connection with cattle. At Dungannon Quarter Sessions in June 1890, before Sir Francis Brady, one farmer sued another for breach of warranty in a cow.[8] It was suggested that the animal was "blinked," or in other words was under the influence of the "evil eye," or had a *pishogue* put upon it. The defendant had agreed to send for the curative charm to a wise woman in the mountains. The *modus operandi* was then proceeded with. Three locks of hair were pulled from the cow's forehead, three from her back, three from her tail, and one from under her nostrils. The directions continued as follows: The operators were to write the names of eight persons in the neighbourhood whom they might suspect of having done the harm (each name three times), and the one of these eight who was considered to be the most likely to have "blinked" the cow was to be pointed out. When this had been done there was to be a bundle of thatch pulled from the roof of the suspected person. The owner of the cow was then to cut a sod, and take a coal out of the fire on a shovel on which to burn the hair, the thatch, and the paper on which the names had been written. The sod was then to be put to the cow's mouth, and if she licked it she would live.

His Honour to defendant: "And did she lick it?"

Defendant: "Ave, lick it; she would have ate it." (Roars of laughter.) It then transpired that the burning of the thatch had been omitted, and this necessitated another journey to the wise woman.

We may also expect to find traces of strange doings with respect to the produce of cows, viz. milk and butter. Various tales are related to the following effect. A herdsman having wounded a hare, which he has discovered sucking one of the cows under his charge, tracks it to a solitary cabin, where he finds an old woman, smeared with blood and gasping for breath, extended almost lifeless on the floor. Similar stories are to be found in England, and helped to make up the witch-element there, though it may be noted that as early as the twelfth century we are informed by Giraldus Cambrensis that certain old hags in Ireland had the power of turning themselves into hares and in that shape sucking cows. The preservation of hares for coursing, which is being taken up in parts of this country, will probably deal the death-blow to this particular superstition. With regard to the stealing of butter many tales are told, of which the following may be taken as an illustration. A priest was walking in his field early one summer's morning when he came upon an old woman gathering the dew from the long grass, and saying, "Come all to me!"

The priest absent-mindedly muttered, "And half to me!" Next morning he discovered in his dairy three times as much butter as he ought to have, while his neighbours complained that they had none at all. On searching the old beldame's house three large tubs of freshly-churned butter were discovered, which, as her entire flocks and herds consisted of a solitary he-goat, left little doubt of her evildoing! [9]

The witch of history is now a thing of the past. No longer does she career on a broomstick to the nocturnal Sabbath, no longer does she sell her soul to the Devil and receive from him in return many signal tokens of his favour, amongst which was generally the gift of a familiar spirit to do her behests. No longer does the judge sentence, no longer does the savage rabble howl execrations at the old witch come to her doom. The witch of history is gone, and can never be rehabilitated—would, that superstition had died with her. For in Ireland, as probably in every part of the civilised world, many things are believed in and practised which seem repugnant to religion and common-sense. Scattered throughout the length and breadth of the land there are to be found persons whom the country-folk credit with the power of performing various extraordinary actions. *From what source* they derive this power is not at all clear—probably neither they themselves nor their devotees have ever set themselves the task of unravelling that psychological problem. Such persons would be extremely insulted if they were termed wizards or witches, and indeed they only represent white witchcraft in a degenerate and colourless stage. Their entire time is not occupied with such work, nor, in the majority of cases, do they take payment for their services; they are ready to practise their art when occasion arises, but apart from such moments they pursue the ordinary avocations of rural life. The gift has come to them either as an accident of birth, or else the especial recipe or charm has descended from father to son, or has been bequeathed to them by the former owner; as a rule such is used for the benefit of their friends.

An acquaintance told the writer some marvellous tales of a man who had the power of stopping bleeding, though the ailing person might be many miles off at the time; he promised to leave the full *modus operandi* to the writer's informant, but the latter was unable to go and see him during his last moments, and so lost the charm, and. as well deprived the writer of the pleasure of satisfying himself as to the efficacy of its working—for in the interests of Science he was fully prepared to cut his finger (slightly) and let the blood flow!

The same informant told the writer of a most respectable woman who had the power of healing sores. Her method is as follows. She thrusts two sally-twigs in the fire until they become red-hot. She then takes one, and makes circles, round the sore (without touching the flesh), all the while repeating a charm, of which the informant, who underwent the process, could not catch the words. When the twig becomes cool, she thrusts it back into the fire, takes out the other, and does as above. The whole process is repeated about ten or twelve times, but not more than two twigs are made use of. She also puts her patients on a certain diet, and this, together with the general air of mystery, no doubt helps to produce the desired results.

Instances also occur in Ireland of persons employing unhallowed means for the purpose of bringing sickness and even death on some one who has fallen foul of them, or else they act on behalf of those whose willingness is circumscribed by their powerlessness. From the Aran Islands a story comes of the power of an old woman to transfer disease from the afflicted individual to another, with the result that the first recovered, while the newly-stricken person died; the passage reads more like the doings of savages in Polynesia or Central Africa than of Christians in Ireland. In 1892 a man stated that a friend of his was sick of an incurable disease, and having been given over by the doctor, sought, after a struggle with his conscience, the services of a *cailleach* who had the power to transfer mortal sickness from the patient to some healthy object who would sicken and die as an unconscious substitute. When fully empowered by her patient, whose honest intention to profit by the unholy remedy was indispensable to its successful working, the *cailleach* would go out into some field close by a public road, and setting herself on her knees she would pluck an herb from the ground, looking out on the road as she did so. The first passer-by her baleful glance lighted upon would take the sick man's disease and die of it in twenty-four hours, the patient mending as the victim sickened and died. [10]

A most extraordinary account of the Black Art, as instanced in the custom known as "burying the sheaf" comes from co. Louth. The narrator states that details are difficult to obtain, at which we are not surprised, but from what he has published the custom appears to be not only exceedingly malignant, but horribly blasphemous. The person working the charm first goes to the chapel, and says certain words with his (or her) back to the altar; then he takes a sheaf of wheat, which he fashions like the human body, sticking pins in the joints of the stems, and (according to one account) shaping a heart of plaited straw. This sheaf he buries, in the name of the Devil, near the house of his enemy, who he believes will gradually pine away as the sheaf decays, dying when it finally decomposes. If the operator of the charm wishes his enemy to die quickly he buries the sheaf in wet ground where it will soon decay; but if on the other hand he desires his victim to linger in pain he chooses a dry spot where decomposition will be slow. Our informant states that a case in which one woman tried to kill another by this means was brought to light in the police court at Ardee a couple of years before he wrote the above account (*i.e.* before 1895). [11]

Though the Statutes against witchcraft in England and Scotland were repealed (the latter very much against the will of the clergy), it is said that that passed by the Irish Parliament was not similarly treated, and consequently is, theoretically, still in force. Be that as it may, it will probably be news to our readers to learn that witchcraft is still officially recognised in Ireland as an offence against the law. In the Commission of the Peace the newly-appointed magistrate is empowered to take cognisance of, amongst other crimes, "Witchcraft, Inchantment, Sorcery, Magic Arts," a curious relic of bygone times to find in the twentieth century, though it is more than unlikely that any Bench in Ireland will ever have to adjudicate in such a case.

In the foregoing pages we have endeavoured to trace the progress of witchcraft in Ireland from its first appearance to the present day, and as well have introduced some subjects which bear indirectly on the question. From the all too few examples to be obtained we have noted its gradual rise to the zenith (which is represented by the period 1661-1690), and from thence its downward progress to the strange beliefs of the day, which in some respects are the degenerate descendants of the witch craft-conception, in others represent ideas older than civilisation. We may pay the tribute of a tearful smile to the ashes of witchcraft, and express our opinion of the present-day beliefs of the simple country-folk by a pitying smile, feeling an the time how much more enlightened we are than those who believed, or still believe, in such absurdities! But the mind of man is built in water-tight compartments. What better embodies the spirit of the young twentieth century than a powerful motor car, fully equipped with the most up-to-date appliances for increasing speed or lessening vibration; in its tuneful hum as it travels at forty-five miles an hour without an effort, we hear the triumph-song of mind over matter. The owner certainly does not believe in witchcraft or *pishogues* (or perhaps in anything save himself!), yet he fastens on the radiator a "Teddy Bear" or some such thing by way of a mascot. Ask him why he does it—he cannot tell, except that others do the same, while all the time at the back of his mind there exists almost unconsciously the belief that such a thing will help to keep him from the troubles and annoyances that beset the path of the motorist. The connection between cause and effect is unknown to him; he cannot tell you why a Teddy Bear will keep the engine from overheating or prevent punctures—and in this respect he is for the moment on exactly the same intellectual level as., let us say, his brother-man of New Zealand, who carries a baked yam with him at night to scare away ghosts.

The truth of the matter is that we all have a vein of superstition in us, which makes its appearance at some period in our lives under one form or another. A. will laugh to scorn B.'s belief in witches or ghosts, while he himself would not undertake a piece of business on a Friday for all the wealth of Crœsus; while C., who laughs at both, will offer his hand to the palmist in full assurance of faith. Each of us dwells in his own particular glass house, and so cannot afford to hurl missiles at his neighbours; milk-magic or motor-mascots, pishogues or palmistry, the method of manifestation is of little account in comparison with the underlying superstition. The latter is an unfortunate trait that has been handed down to us from the infancy of the race; we have managed to get rid of such physical features as tails or third eyes, whose day of usefulness has passed; we no longer masticate our meat raw, or chip the rugged flint into the semblance of a knife, but we still acknowledge our descent by giving expression to the strange beliefs that lie in some remote lumber-room at the back of the brain.

But it may be objected that belief in witches, ghosts, fairies, charms, evil-eye, &c. &c., need not be put down as unreasoning superstition, pure and simple, that in fact the trend of modern thought is to show us that there are more things in heaven and earth than were formerly dreamt of. We grant that man is a very complex machine, a microcosm peopled with possibilities of which we can understand but little. We know that mind acts on mind to an extraordinary degree, and that the imagination can affect the body to an extent not yet fully realised, and indeed has often carried men far beyond the bounds of common-sense; and so we consider that many of the elements of the above beliefs can in a general way be explained along these lines. Nevertheless that does not do away with the element of superstition and, we may add, oftentimes of deliberately-planned evil that underlies. There is no need to resurrect the old dilemma, whether God or the Devil was the principal agent concerned; we have no desire to preach to our readers, but we feel that every thinking man will be fully prepared to admit that such beliefs and practices are inimical to the development of true spiritual life, in that they tend to obscure the ever-present Deity and bring into prominence primitive feelings and emotions which are better left to fall into a state of atrophy. In addition they cripple the growth of national life, as they make the individual the fearful slave of the unknown, and consequently prevent the development of an independent spirit in him without which a nation is only such in name. The dead past utters warnings to the heirs of all the ages. It tells us already we have partially entered into a glorious heritage, which may perhaps be as nothing in respect of what will ultimately fall to the lot of the human race, and it bids us give our upward-soaring spirits freedom, and not fetter them with the gross beliefs of yore that should long ere this have been relegated to limbo.

Footnotes

1. In the shorter version of the poem this line runs—

"He cured the kye for Nanny Barton,"

which makes better sense. Huie Mertin was evidently a rival of Mary Butters.

1. South-running water possessed great healing qualities. See Dalyell, *Darker Superstitions of Scotland*, and C. K. Sharpe, *op. cit.* p. 94.
2. When a child the writer often heard that if a man were led astray at night by Jacky-the-Lantern (or John Barleycorn, or any other potent sprite!), the best way to get home safely was to turn one's coat inside out and wear it in that condition.
3. *Notes and Queries*, 4th series, vol. vii.
4. Henderson, *Folklore of Northern Counties of England*, (Folklore Society).
5. *Journal of Royal Society of Antiquaries of Ireland*, xxii. (consec. ser.), p. 291.
6. *Irish Times* for 14th June; *Independent* for 1st July.
7. *Journal of Royal Society of Antiquaries of Ireland*, xxi. (consec. ser.), pp. 406-7.
8. *Folklore*.
9. *Journal of Royal Society of Antiquaries of Ireland*, xxv. (consec. ser.) p. 84.
10. *Folklore*, vi. 302

CPSIA information can be obtained
at www.ICGtesting.com
Printed in the USA
LVHW080323140921
697765LV00002B/20